BARACK
OBAMA

Look for more fascinating biographies in the series!

Hillary Clinton
George W. Bush
Steve Jobs
Nelson Mandela
Sally Ride

A REAL-LIFE STORY

BARACK OBAMA

OUR FORTY-FOURTH PRESIDENT

by BEATRICE GORMLEY

ALADDIN
New York   London   Toronto   Sydney   New Delhi

To my husband, Bob

ALADDIN

An imprint of Simon & Schuster Children's Publishing Division

1230 Avenue of the Americas, New York, New York 10020

This Aladdin paperback edition March 2017

Text copyright © 2008, 2012, 2105 by Beatrice Gormley

Cover photograph copyright © 2015 by Allen Tannenbaum–Pool/Getty Images

Also available in an Aladdin hardcover edition.

For information about special discounts for bulk purchases, please contact Simon & Schuster Special Sales at 1-866-506-1949 or business@simonandschuster.com.

The Simon & Schuster Speakers Bureau can bring authors to your live event. For more information or to book an event contact the Simon & Schuster Speakers Bureau at 1-866-248-3049 or visit our website at www.simonspeakers.com.

Book designed by Karina Granda

The text of this book was set in Bembo STD.

Manufactured in the United States of America 0217 OFF

2 4 6 8 10 9 7 5 3 1

Library of Congress Control Number 2015937914

ISBN 978-1-4814-4648-8 (hc)

ISBN 978-1-4814-4649-5 (pbk)

ISBN 978-1-4814-4650-1 (eBook)

CONTENTS

CHAPTER 1

BARACK OBAMA JR.

ON AUGUST 4, 1961, A BABY BOY WAS BORN AT Kapiʻolani Medical Center in Honolulu, Hawaii. He weighed eight pounds, two ounces. His parents, Ann and Barack, named him after his father, Barack Hussein Obama, but they called their child "Barry."

Barack Obama Sr. was a foreign exchange student from Kenya, a country in east-central Africa. He was twenty-five years old, studying on a scholarship at the University of Hawaii. He was the very first African student at the school.

Barack was tall and charming, with a voice "like black velvet," as his mother-in-law Madelyn Dunham described it, "with a British accent." He had come from a poor family, herding goats as a boy. His father, of the Luo tribe, had been a domestic servant for the British colonials. Now Kenya was on the brink of gaining independence from Britain.

Barack was determined to accomplish great things, both for himself and for his country. It was a great honor for a youth from his humble background to study at American schools and earn an advanced degree in economics. But he also had a heavy responsibility to his people, and he intended to return to Kenya and help lead the country into a brighter future.

Ann Dunham was an eighteen-year-old freshman at the University of Hawaii in 1960 when she met Barack in a Russian class. A quiet but independent-minded girl, she had dark curly hair and dark eyebrows like her father's. She read serious books about reforming society, and she eagerly spent hours in long, earnest discussions with her friends.

Ann lived with her parents, Stanley and Madelyn Dunham, in a rambling house near the university campus. Stanley was a furniture salesman, while Madelyn worked for a bank. Both Stanley and Madelyn had grown up in Kansas, but after they married, they lived in several states before settling in Hawaii.

When Ann first brought Barack home for dinner, her parents, especially Madelyn, were uneasy. They had never met anyone from Africa before. But Barack quickly won them over with his charm, and they were impressed with his brilliant mind and his confidence.

However, the Dunhams were unpleasantly surprised in February 1961, when Ann and Barack eloped to the island of Maui and came back married. Stanley and Madelyn were disappointed that Ann, so bright and inquisitive of mind, was dropping out of college after only one semester. Madelyn also feared that the cultural differences between their American daughter and this African young man were too great.

Barack's father, Hussein Onyango Obama, who lived in Kenya, was also surprised and very upset at the news. He threatened to get Barack's travel visa canceled, so he'd have to return to Kenya. He pointed out that Barack already had family responsibilities: a wife and two children in Kenya. Also, he warned his son, an American wife wasn't likely to be understanding about the Kenyan custom of a man having more than one family. Furthermore, Onyango wrote Stanley Dunham a long, angry letter. As Barry's mother told him years later, Barack's father "didn't want the Obama blood sullied by a white woman."

Barack refused to obey his father, and the Dunhams accepted their daughter's choice. For two years Barack and Ann lived with their baby in a small white house near the university campus. Then in 1963, Barack graduated from the University of Hawaii and won a scholarship to study economics at Harvard University in Massachusetts. The scholarship didn't allow enough money to bring Ann and their son with him, but Barack felt he couldn't pass up the chance to study at such a prestigious university. In the end, he left Hawaii for Massachusetts by himself.

Barack Sr. intended to eventually take his wife and son back to Kenya, after he had earned his PhD in economics. But Ann decided that this marriage would not work. Barack might love her and Barry, but his wife and son were not as important as his fierce ambition or his commitment to Kenya. Besides, it did matter to Ann, as Barack's father had predicted, that Barack had a wife and children in Kenya. In January 1964, she filed for divorce.

During his first years, Barry didn't wonder why his father was missing. Family pictures show him happily riding his tricycle or perched on a fence with his mother's arm around him. In another picture from those days, Barry frolics in the surf with his grandfather Stanley (whom Barry called "Gramps"). A boisterous, outgoing man, Stanley was delighted to have Barry to play with and show off to friends and neighbors. Madelyn Dunham was more practical and sensible, but she too doted on their grandson. She told him to call her "Tutu," Hawaiian for "grandmother," and the name got shortened to "Toot."

Barry's mother and grandparents talked to him about his father, but they never criticized Barack Sr. to Barry. Ann especially must have felt pain and anger over the failed marriage, but she didn't say anything to Barry about that. The worst thing she said about Barack Obama was that he was a terrible driver.

Ann told Barry that he had a wonderful father— fiercely intelligent, with a deep baritone voice and a way of commanding people's attention. She showed him pictures of Barack Sr., a dark-skinned man with glasses. She told him his father loved him very much.

Although Barry wouldn't realize it for many years, his mother was just as remarkable as his father. Her full name was Stanley Ann Dunham, because her father had wished for a son. Growing up, she didn't like having a boy's name, but feeling different from other children may have made her more independent as well.

Once, when the Dunhams were living in Texas, Ann brought a black friend home to play. That would have been fine with Ann's parents, but the neighborhood children taunted the girls with racial slurs, driving the black girl away. Even more disturbing, the adult townspeople blamed the incident on the Dunhams. Instead of scolding their own children, they advised the Dunhams not to let Ann associate with black playmates.

When Ann was in the eighth grade, the family moved to Seattle, Washington. Stanley was offered a better job in a furniture store there, and they were all glad to leave Texas. Madelyn found a job in a bank. In 1956, the Dunhams bought a house on Mercer Island, near Seattle, so that Ann could attend the new high school there.

Ann was an idealistic and curious girl, with a mind of her own. Some of her high school friends were surprised that she didn't feel any need to fit in with other young people. She didn't seem to have the usual interest in dating or eventually getting married and having children.

What did interest Ann were current events and the controversial ideas set forth by her English and philosophy teachers. These teachers angered many in the community by questioning religion, the U.S. political system, and other parts of the American way of life. Some of the thought-provoking books they assigned were Vance Packard's *The Hidden Persuaders*, about the power of advertising; George Orwell's *1984*, a novel about a grim future in which the countries of the world are always at war and the government controls citizens' minds with lies and violence; and William Whyte's *The Organization Man*, which described big American corporations as controlling every aspect of their employees' lives.

Ann and her friends had long discussions on such topics after school in coffee shops. She spent much of her free time reading. She was fascinated with other cultures, and she was idealistic about how people's lives could be improved.

Toward the end of her high school career, Ann applied to the University of Chicago and received early acceptance. The University of Chicago, with its reputation for intellectual excitement, in the middle of a big city, appealed to Ann's sense of adventure. However, Stanley Dunham didn't want his daughter living on her own, far away from home, at such a young age.

After Ann's graduation from high school, in 1960, Stanley heard that a new opportunity was opening up in the furniture business in Honolulu. Always ready for a new adventure and hopeful for a better life somewhere else, he decided to move the family to Hawaii.

Ann resented her father for running her life, and she

was reluctant to leave Seattle. But Hawaii wasn't such a bad place to be: a land of warm, sandy beaches and transparent blue water, of steep rain forest–covered hills with water-falls and ginger flowers. Also, in Hawaii, Ann encountered people with an interesting mix of backgrounds: Japanese, Filipino, Polynesian. Ann enrolled in the University of Hawaii to study anthropology. She soon fell in with a group of students who shared her interest in politics and world affairs. One of them—the one with the most forceful, confident opinions—was Barack Obama.

After divorcing Barack in 1964, Ann went back to school at the University of Hawaii. She had no money, but she got by with food stamps and with her parents' help. While Ann was in class, Barry's grandparents took care of him.

Ann soon met another foreign exchange student she liked very much, an Indonesian man named Lolo Soetoro. Indonesia, like Kenya, was a recently independent country. Lolo's father and brother had both died in the struggle against the Dutch colonialists, and the Dutch army had burned their house. Lolo was proud of his country and wanted to con-tribute to building a better Indonesia. He planned to teach at the university when he returned to Jakarta, the capital city.

Having a much more easygoing personality than

Barack Sr., Lolo got along well with the Dunhams. He enjoyed tussling with young Barry and playing chess with Stanley. Lolo wanted to remain in Hawaii until he finished his studies, but Indonesia in the mid-1960s was a country in turmoil.

President Sukarno had ruled Indonesia since the declaration of independence in 1945, but there was increasing unrest against his government. In 1965 the army led a violent anti-communist purge in which hundreds of thousands died. In 1966, Lolo was ordered back to Indonesia to serve in the army. He and Ann decided to marry before he left, with the plan that she and Barry would join him several months later.

Stanley was excited for Ann and Barry, moving to a place more exotic than Hawaii, with tigers and monsoons. Madelyn was worried that the country might not be safe for them, because of the political upheaval. Ann and Barry needed to get shots and passports, since they'd never left the United States before. In 1967 they boarded a plane to fly first to Japan and then to Jakarta, Indonesia, about a third of the way around the globe from Hawaii.

CHAPTER 2

INDONESIA

BOTH HAWAII AND INDONESIA ARE TROPICAL archipelagoes, or chains of islands, but there the resemblance ends. Indonesia, including the principal islands of Java, Borneo, Sumatra, and Bali, is a hundred times greater in land area than Hawaii. At the time Barry and his family lived in Indonesia, its population was well over 100 million, while Hawaii's population was around 700,000. Even the weather is different. In Honolulu, although the temperature is usually very warm, the constant trade winds make it feel comfortable. Jakarta, lying right near the equator, is extremely hot and steamy.

Six-year-old Barry Obama and his mother were thrilled with the adventure of living in an entirely strange place. As Lolo drove them home from the airport the first day, he pointed out a towering statue of Hanuman the

monkey god. At Lolo's house Barry found baby croco-
diles in the backyard, as well as an ape, specially bought
as a pet for Barry. Birds of paradise, trailing extravagant
plumage, perched in the trees. There were also chickens in
the backyard—and one of them, Barry was astounded to
learn, would be slaughtered for their dinner.

The Indonesian language was incomprehensible to
Barry at first, and he didn't know anyone except his mother
and stepfather. However, Lolo's relatives were warm and
welcoming to his American wife and stepson. In the
neighborhood, Barry set out to make friends. Perching on
the garden wall, he flapped his arms and cawed like a crow
to make the other children laugh.

Soon Barry was kicking a soccer ball around with the
other children. There was no end of exciting things to do:
playing in rice paddies, riding on water buffalo, flying kites
in fierce contests. He learned to eat unfamiliar things like
tofu and tempeh, spiced with hot peppers. He learned to
expect the teachers at his new school to lash him with a
bamboo switch if he misbehaved. Lolo, a caring stepfather,
taught Barry how to defend himself if another boy picked
a fight.

One of the strangest things about Indonesia, for both

Ann and Barry, was the poverty. Although Lolo's house had no electricity, it was a comfortable white stucco house with a red tiled roof. But many of their neighbors lived in bamboo huts. The neighboring farmers might lose their whole year's crop if there was a drought, and they were helpless against severe floods.

And then there were hordes of beggars: homeless, jobless, orphaned, blind, deformed, or with hideous diseases like leprosy. Ann was so tenderhearted that her eyes filled with tears and her chin trembled at the sight of these truly destitute people. She wanted to help everyone who came to the door and asked for money.

But Lolo had a different attitude. He told Barry that life was hard, and that was just the way it was. He gave hints about what *he* had endured the year that General Suharto's government yanked him away from his studies in Hawaii and sent him into the swamps of New Guinea to fight the communist rebels. He showed Barry the scars on his legs where he'd dug leeches out with a hot knife.

It was impractical, Lolo explained, to try to help everyone who needed help. It was hard enough just to take care of yourself and your family. Lolo was lucky to be educated and have a job, working for the army as a geologist. He intended to get a better job and move up in the world.

Lolo was Muslim, although not very devout. He sometimes went to the mosque to pray, and once in a long while he took Barry with him. Islam, as many Indonesians practiced it, included elements of Hinduism, such as the monkey god Hanuman, as well as bits of the religion of the original Indonesian tribes. Everyone in Lolo's neighborhood was Muslim, but Ann and Lolo sent Barry to a Catholic school, Franciscus Assisi Primary School. All the children there, including Barry, were expected to take part in the daily Catholic prayers, although it was merely a rote exercise to Barry.

At school, as in his neighborhood, Barry didn't see anyone who looked like him. This was different from Hawaii, where the population was a mix of various ethnic groups: the Polynesians who first settled the islands, the white Europeans who arrived in the eighteenth century, the Asians who began immigrating there in the nineteenth century, and many other groups who'd arrived since. Here all the children were short, slight Indonesians—except for tall, husky Barry. His skin was darker than theirs, and his hair was curly rather than straight.

Barry had to work to learn the new language, and he

was sometimes teased for being a foreigner and different-looking. Once a friend tricked him into eating a piece of shrimp paste, telling him it was chocolate. At least Barry knew the Indonesian word for this situation. *"Curang, curang!"* he shouted at the other boy, spitting out the shrimp paste. "Cheater, cheater!"

But Barry, a cheerful and outgoing boy, wasn't discouraged by the teasing. He was naturally kind, protecting smaller children and helping up anyone who fell down. His first-grade teacher, Israella Darmawan, noticed how bright he was, and how the other children tended to follow his lead.

Meanwhile, Ann took a job as an English teacher at the U.S. embassy in Jakarta. She was already tutoring Barry in English, waking him up early to study before school every morning. While Ann wanted Barry to adapt to Indonesia, she didn't want him to lose ground in his native language.

In 1970, Ann gave birth to a daughter, Maya Kassandra Soetoro. She taught Maya from an early age, as she had Barry, that everyone was the same under the skin. All people had the right to be respected. Maya's doll collection looked "like the United Nations," as she said later. There was a black doll, an Inuit doll, a Dutch doll.

14

Barry's mother coached him to be proud of his own special identity. She taught him about Dr. Martin Luther King Jr. and the civil rights movement and about Supreme Court Justice Thurgood Marshall and the historic changes in U.S. laws about race. She played Mahalia Jackson's gospel music for him.

She also taught him that his African father was a man of high ideals. Barack Sr. had grown up poor, but he would never go along with a corrupt system just because it was the practical thing to do. Barry was like his father, she told him, and she was sure he would follow his father's example.

From his mother Barry got the impression that being part black was something to be proud of. However, when he was around nine years old, he came across a magazine article that disturbed him deeply.

It was about an American black man who had tried to lighten his skin with a "miracle" cream. Pictures in the article showed how the chemicals had left his skin patchy and disfigured. It was horrible that the treatment had turned out badly, but it seemed even worse to Barry that the man had wanted so desperately to be white. Barry didn't talk to anyone about this, but it started him thinking.

Lolo was now working for Mobil Oil as a government

relations consultant, a well-paying job. In 1970 he was able to buy a house in a better neighborhood, where the streets were paved and the houses were securely walled off from beggars and thieves. Barry had now studied at the Catholic school for three years, but after the family moved he began attending a government-run school.

This school, State Elementary School Menteng 1, offered religious instruction once a week. Barry was registered as Muslim, because his stepfather was considered Muslim, so he attended the Muslim class. He sometimes made faces during the study of the Koran, which meant no more to him than the prayers at his Catholic school had. When his teacher complained to his mother, Ann explained to Barry that he should be respectful of others' beliefs and behave himself during religion class. Ann wasn't at all religious, but she thought it was good for children to be exposed to different faiths.

Outside religion classes, the government school encouraged the children to celebrate the holidays of other religions as well as Islam. They put up decorations for both Christmas and Eid al-Adha, an Islamic holiday. Unlike the custom at traditional Muslim schools, the boys and girls were not separated, and the girls did not wear head scarves.

Many of the women teachers wore Western-style clothes such as sleeveless dresses.

Barry's new school was supposed to be one of the best in Jakarta, but Ann was dissatisfied with the education he was getting. She was afraid her early morning English lessons with Barry wouldn't make up for second-rate schooling. Barry seemed to be spending too much of the school day sitting in the back of the classroom drawing superheroes, like Batman and Spider-Man. Ann worried more and more about the limited opportunities he would have if he stayed in Indonesia.

Then there was the time Barry came home with a long, deep gash in his arm. Playing on a mud slide with a friend, he'd ripped his arm open on a barbed-wire fence. Barry wasn't worried about the injury, and neither was his stepfather, but Ann borrowed a car and rushed Barry to the hospital. Even the two doctors at the hospital weren't very concerned. They finished their game of dominoes before sewing Barry's wound up with twenty stitches. The incident caused Ann to realize that her son might not receive proper medical care in this country.

She was concerned about Barry's values, too. In Jakarta, corruption and going along with the unfair system were

17

facts of life. When she and Barry first arrived at the Jakarta airport, Lolo bribed the customs guards so that they didn't have to wait in the long lines. When the tax officials came to inspect Lolo's house, he hid the refrigerator so that it wouldn't be counted on his tax bill.

Everyone in Indonesia did their best to get around inconvenient rules, but Ann didn't want Barry's character formed by such attitudes. She wanted him to value honesty, fairness, and independent judgment, as her parents had taught her. A hard life wasn't an excuse for low standards. Look at Barack Obama Sr., who came from a poor, uneducated family but still dedicated his life to working for the benefit of the Kenyan people.

Some of Ann's teachings must have rubbed off on Barry. His third-grade teacher, Fermina Sinaga, later remembered an essay he wrote about what he wanted to be when he grew up. "He wanted to be president," she said. "He didn't say what country he wanted to be president of. But he wanted to make everybody happy."

In the summer of 1970, Barry flew back to Hawaii to spend his vacation with his grandparents. They, too, were concerned about Barry's education, and they took him to interview at Punahou School, a prestigious private school

in Honolulu. In the summer of 1971, Ann sent Barry back
to Hawaii to begin attending Punahou in the fall. For the
time being, he would live with his grandparents.

As for Ann, she promised to join Barry within a year,
maybe by Christmas. Ann was disappointed in Lolo. When
she fell in love with him in Hawaii, he'd had high ideals
about a life of service to the Indonesian people. She had
thought they would work together to improve his country.
But he had given up his ideals, while she felt more and more
deeply for the poor people of Indonesia. Ann and Lolo had
drifted apart, and this marriage, too, would soon end.

CHAPTER 3

BACK TO HAWAII

BARRY'S GRANDPARENTS MADELYN AND STANLEY had begun their marriage with an elopement, just as his mother and father had done. Madelyn's parents were conventional, respectable citizens of Augusta, Kansas, and Stanley Dunham was an adventurous young man from El Dorado with a salesman's charm and a bad reputation. Madelyn's parents had disapproved of him even more than the Dunhams later disapproved of the African graduate student Barack Obama. So Stanley and Madelyn had gotten married secretly, a few weeks before Madelyn graduated from high school in 1940.

Ann, the Dunhams' only child, had been born in Fort Leavenworth, Kansas, in 1942, during World War II. Stanley Dunham was in the army at the time, and he was shipped off to France to fight under General Patton.

Madelyn worked at the Boeing aircraft plant in Wichita.

After the end of World War II in 1945, the Dunhams moved around the country: California, Texas, Kansas, and the state of Washington. Madelyn and Stanley weren't especially aware of the racial discrimination that was common everywhere in the United States at that time. However, they believed in being polite and considerate to everyone, and they were appalled at the harsh racial segregation they found in Texas.

When Madelyn spoke politely to the black janitor at the bank where she worked, a fellow employee scolded her sharply for doing so. At the store where Stanley sold furniture, the other salesmen explained to him that African-Americans and Mexicans were not allowed in the store during regular hours. They could buy furniture, but they had to look at it after hours, when there were no white customers in the store.

When the Dunhams finally settled in Hawaii in 1960, they appreciated the multicultural way of life in the islands. In Hawaii, whites had always been in the minority, and many in the population were of mixed race. The Dunhams shopped at a neighborhood market run by a Japanese American; they were invited over for poi and roast pig by native Hawaiian fellow employees of Stanley's; Stanley played checkers in the park with old Filipino men.

In 1971, when Barry returned from Indonesia to attend school in Honolulu, Stanley and Madelyn Dunham were eager to do everything they could for their grandson. Stanley's employer, a Punahou School alumnus, had helped by recommending Barry for admission. The school accepted Barry and gave him a partial scholarship, but his family had to pay the rest of his tuition.

Ann, in the process of separating from Lolo, had no money to spare. Barry's grandparents didn't have much more. They moved from their large house near the University of Hawaii campus to a two-bedroom apartment. Stanley Dunham now worked as a life insurance salesman, a job he disliked and didn't do well at. Fortunately, Madelyn had been promoted to vice president at the Bank of Hawaii, so she could manage to pay the balance of Barry's tuition fees.

Stanley and Madelyn Dunham were proud that Barry was attending Punahou, a high-ranking college-preparatory school founded in 1841. Besides its academic excellence, Punahou boasted a beautiful, secluded campus, with several acres of broad lawns and shady paths. Green hills overlooked the classroom buildings, theaters, tennis courts, and swimming pools.

After four years in Indonesia, Barry felt like an outsider at first. His classmates all knew one another, having attended Punahou since kindergarten. Barry seemed to be wearing the wrong clothes, and his classmates played football—the soccer he'd played in Indonesia wouldn't become a popular sport in the United States for years. The other students came mainly from well-to-do families. While Barry and his grandparents lived in a nondescript concrete high-rise apartment building, most of his classmates lived in spacious houses with backyard swimming pools.

At the age of six, the last time Barry had lived in Honolulu, he'd felt perfectly comfortable as part of Hawaii's ethnic melting pot. His grandfather Stanley used to tease tourists on the beach by telling them with a straight face that Barry was the great-grandson of the Hawaiian king Kamehameha. He thought it was a great joke when they solemnly took a picture of the boy playing in the sand to paste in their photo albums back home.

But now ten-year-old Barry was more aware of racial differences and discrimination. He began to notice that there weren't many African-Americans in Hawaii. In

Barry's fifth-grade class, there was only one other black child, a girl. A few of the students at Punahou were of Asian heritage, but most of them were white.

During Barry's first semester, his mother did join him in Honolulu as she'd promised. But much more momentous, Barry learned that he was going to meet a man he'd been hearing about for years: his own father. Barack Sr. was coming to Hawaii for a month at Christmastime 1971 to visit his American son. The Dunhams arranged for him to stay in an apartment in their building.

Barry had last seen Barack Obama Sr. when he was two years old, too young to remember. He knew he was supposed to be delighted about seeing his father, but instead he felt confused and resentful. He learned that his father had married again for the third time and had six other children—five boys and a girl—in Kenya.

Over the years Ann had worked hard to build up the bond between Barry and his father. Ann had written many letters to Barack about Barry, and she'd always praised her ex-husband to Barry. Stanley, too, had talked about Barry's father as a supremely confident, commanding man.

Now Ann assured Barry that he and his father would be "great friends," and she tried to prepare him for the visit with information about Kenya. The country had gained independence from British rule in 1963, under the leadership of Jomo Kenyatta, who was still the president in 1971. Kenya was a mixture of many different ethnic groups. While Jomo Kenyatta was from the Kikuyu tribe, Barack Sr. was from the Luo tribe. The Luo had come to Kenya several hundred years earlier from the Nile River region.

Barry didn't pay close attention, but he got the impression that his father's tribe had originally come from ancient Egypt. That sounded exciting, and at first he was eager to learn more about the Luo. But then Barry read in a library book that the Luo were cattle-herders who lived in mud huts. This was nothing like the pyramids and chariots he'd hoped for. Ashamed, he didn't want to know any more.

When Barack Sr. finally arrived in Honolulu, Barry still felt confused. His father was tall and very thin. He walked with a cane, because he was recovering from a car accident. As the visit went on, Barry still felt uncomfortable around his father and found it hard to talk to him. They were strangers.

Barry did notice how his mother and grandparents responded to Barack. Something magnetic about him seemed to liven up the air when he was in the room.

At first, the four adults enjoyed one another's company, and everyone got along. But after a few weeks, tensions built up.

One evening Barry started to watch a children's Christmas special on TV, *How the Grinch Stole Christmas!* Barack Sr. ordered him to turn the TV off and study instead. Barry's father assumed he had the authority to give such commands, but his mother and grandmother protested. The adults began to argue bitterly, no longer trying to be polite, while Barry listened from the other room.

Barack accused Barry's grandparents of spoiling him. Stanley was indignant that Barack would try to take charge in *his* house. Madelyn thought her ex-son-in-law had some nerve to come there and give orders, when he'd left Ann and their little son to fend for themselves eight years ago. (She didn't add that she worked full-time at the bank, and she was tired of waiting on Barack.) Ann, who wanted everyone to love and understand one another, reproached Barack for being too tough with Barry, and her parents for never changing.

After this scene, Barry just wanted his father to leave so that he and his mother and grandparents could return to their peaceful life. But then Barry's teacher invited Barack Sr. to come to Punahou and talk to the fifth graders about Kenya. At first Barry dreaded the visit. Besides the fact that he felt uncomfortable around his father, he was afraid Barack Sr. wouldn't measure up to the heroic reputation Barry had created for him. Barry had made the mistake of bragging to his classmates that his father was an African prince, and now the truth about the mud huts would come out.

However, on the day that Barack Sr. spoke to the students at Punahou, Barry was proud. His classmates were impressed with his tall father, looking dignified in his blue blazer. Barack spoke to them in his deep, velvety voice of Kenyan legends and of how Kenya gained its independence from British rule. They listened, mesmerized. By the end of the presentation, Barry was smiling.

At Christmas, Barry gave his father a tie, and his father gave him a basketball. And then before he left, Barack Sr. gave his son one last present: a recording of African music. Even better, Barack played the record for Barry and showed him how to dance like a Luo.

When Ann returned to Hawaii to live, she brought Barry's half-sister Maya with her.

She had left Lolo Soetoro, although she would remain

on friendly terms with him, as she had with Barry's father. She applied for student grants so that she could go back to school at the University of Hawaii and support her children. Ann planned to become an anthropologist, a social scientist who studies different cultures. She already knew she wanted to work in Indonesia, which contained a fascinating array of cultures. Some three hundred separate languages were spoken throughout the country.

The summer after his father visited Barry, Madelyn Dunham took him, his mother, and Maya on a tour of the United States. Barry, almost eleven, had never seen the mainland before. They traveled from Seattle, Washington, to California, where they went to Disneyland. In Arizona they viewed the Grand Canyon.

Then they rode the Greyhound bus east across the Midwest, where Madelyn had grown up and Ann had been born. They traveled north to Chicago on Lake Michigan, where they spent three days. On the way back to the West Coast for the flight home, they stopped in Yellowstone Park.

Back in Honolulu, Barry lived with his mother and Maya in an apartment near the Punahou School campus. Ann was close and loving with her children, but she expected them to do their part. Since Ann was a single parent, she needed Barry to help out by grocery shopping and looking after his little sister.

Maya adored her brother, but as she got older she liked to tease him. A young teenager now, Barry was proud of his carefully arranged Afro hairstyle. One way to get a rise out of him, Maya discovered, was to mess up his hair.

In spite of all the studying and chores, there was time for Ann, Barry, and Maya to have fun together. On weekends the family might hike and picnic in the wooded hills above Honolulu, where waterfalls cascaded down mossy cliffs and red ginger flowers dotted the undergrowth. Ann had a reverence for the wonders of nature, and she was eager to share her awe with Barry and Maya. She might go so far as to wake them up in the middle of the night to look at an especially beautiful moon.

In 1977 Ann was ready to return to Indonesia for her fieldwork in anthropology. She intended to take Maya and Barry with her. She was still concerned about her children's education, but she planned to send them to a good school in Jakarta, the International School.

Since Ann loved the people and culture of Indonesia, she looked forward to the move, and Maya didn't object.

But Barry wanted to stay in Hawaii. He was now in high school at Punahou, and he didn't want to leave his friends. Stanley and Madelyn encouraged Barry to stay, offering to let him have one of their two small bedrooms. Also, although they didn't exactly say so, they let Barry understand that they wouldn't supervise him as strictly as his mother did.

Ann hated the thought of parting with Barry, but she understood how he felt. He had made a big adjustment to Indonesia at the age of six, and then another big adjustment to Hawaii at the age of ten. Naturally he didn't want to go back to Indonesia and readjust all over again.

So Ann and Maya left, and Barry moved in with his grandparents. He would live there until he graduated from high school two years later.

CHAPTER 4

HIGH SCHOOL

DURING HIS HIGH SCHOOL YEARS AT PUNAHOU, Barry's classmates thought of him as a warm, friendly, low-key kind of guy with a great smile. Bigger than most of his classmates, Barry played football during his freshman year. But he loved basketball more, and that was his main sport throughout high school. He played second string on the varsity team.

Barry's mother, perhaps remembering how serious she'd been as a teenager, wondered if Barry would ever care about anything except basketball. But Barry was like his mother in at least one way—his sense of fairness. As in elementary school in Indonesia, he was genuinely kind. His classmates noticed that he would refuse to go along with the crowd in teasing another student. Standing apart, Barry would give the tormentors a look of disapproval.

In basketball, Barry was a solid, steady player, although not a star. His sense of fairness came out in sports, too. If the coach was keeping the second-string players on the bench too long, Barry would be the one to speak up for them.

Barry's grades were decent, but not outstanding, and his classmates and teachers knew that he could have been a top student with a little more effort. The good life in Hawaii may have had something to do with Barry's lack of seriousness. Hawaii, more than two thousand miles from the mainland United States, seemed peacefully removed from the rest of the world. The weather was always pleasant, the scenery beautiful.

For Barry and his friends, life was an endless round of bodysurfing at Sandy Beach, going to parties, and playing basketball. Besides the varsity games and practice, they played pickup basketball with the young men who showed up at the gym after school. Barry also spent hours practicing basketball shots by himself on a playground near his grandparents' apartment.

There were a few small signs that Barry was an unusual boy. He read a lot of books, and he listened to jazz artists such as Miles Davis and Charlie Parker as well as the pop music that his classmates liked. Once, he surprised the other students in an English class with a poem he wrote. It was about "an old, forgotten man on an old, forgotten road" who "walks a straight line along the crooked world."

In fact, although Barry didn't talk to his friends about it, he was on an identity quest. As he grew up, he also grew more aware of himself as an American with African ancestry, and he searched for a group to identify with. Who was he?

For one thing, Barry was the son of a black African father. His mother had always emphasized what a remarkable, admirable man her first husband was and encouraged Barry to be like him. Barry did think of his father as a kind of hero.

But he had seen his father only once to remember, when he was ten. His father wrote him letters, and Barry wrote back, but they weren't close the way Barry and his mother were. Barry hadn't even met any of his other African relatives, and he certainly didn't feel African.

However, although Barry was close to his white American mother and white American grandparents, he certainly didn't feel white, either. Was he African-American, then? But he had no African-American family or community.

Barry searched in books to find out who he was and where he belonged. He read all the well-known writers on the struggles of black people in America: W. E. B. DuBois's essays in *The Souls of Black Folk*, Langston Hughes's poems, the novelists Richard Wright (*Native Son*) and Ralph Waldo Ellison (*Invisible Man*), Dr. Martin Luther King Jr.'s speeches, James Baldwin's essays in *The Fire Next Time*, and Malcolm X's *The Autobiography of Malcolm X*.

The African-American writer who appealed to Barry most of all at that time in his life was Malcolm X, with his dignity, his confidence, and his stern call for justice. Barry was also deeply impressed at how Malcolm had been able to turn his life around. Still, it bothered him that Malcolm completely rejected his white background on his mother's side. It was one thing for Malcolm, who had never known his white grandfather, to disavow his white family; it would be quite another for Barry to reject his close and loving mother and grandparents, who had cared for him all his life.

Barry knew that because he lived in Hawaii, he wasn't experiencing the same discrimination that most African-Americans faced. Of all the fifty states, Hawaii was the most tolerant of racial differences. Barry's own father had said so, Barry discovered. Barry found a clipping, an article the *Honolulu Star-Bulletin* had published in 1963, when his father graduated from the University of Hawaii. At the time Barack Sr. had noted that other nations could learn something from the way the different races in Hawaii were willing to cooperate.

Stanley Dunham liked to tell a story from the days when Barack Sr. was still attending the University of Hawaii. One evening Barry's father and Stanley had gone with a group of friends to a bar in Waikiki. While they were having drinks, a white customer in the bar started to complain loudly about Barack Sr.'s presence, using racial slurs.

Barry's father, instead of starting a fight, walked over to the white man with a calm smile. With great dignity and authority he explained to the other man that racial discrimination was wrong, foolish, and against the American principle of respecting the rights of everyone. The white man was so ashamed, Stanley said, that he not only stopped complaining but also pulled a hundred dollars out of his pocket and pressed the money on Barack.

Barack's confidence would have been a lot more reassuring, Barry thought, if his father were here. Meanwhile, Barry couldn't help noticing some evidence of racism even in Hawaii. His tennis coach, for instance, had made a snide remark about Barry's color.

As far as the coach was concerned, Barry didn't have any mixed feelings. He thought the guy was a jerk, and he quit the tennis team. But he was more confused when it came to friends and family. One night when Barry took two white friends to an all-black party, they felt uncomfortable, and before long they asked him to drive them home. In the car one of the friends tried to tell Barry that he now understood a little bit of what Barry must feel all the time, being surrounded by white people.

Instead of appreciating his friend's sympathy, Barry became angry. How could the white boy possibly understand how he felt? Whites were in charge in this society. If they felt uncomfortable, they could just leave the party; whereas if Barry felt uncomfortable, he could do nothing about it.

Then there was the time Barry's grandmother was harassed at a bus stop by a panhandler. Barry's grandfather told him privately, with shame, that his grandmother had been frightened because the man was black. Barry was shaken to think that his own Toot was afraid of someone just on the basis of his being African-American. Later, however, an older black man named Frank suggested a different view to Barry. In Frank's opinion, Barry's grandmother wasn't really wrong to react that way. Considering the long history of racial bigotry in the United States, African-Americans had a reason to harbor deep anger against whites. And such anger sometimes led to violence against whites.

Gramps's attitude bothered Barry, too. Stanley Dunham thought of himself as completely free of racial prejudice. It was true that Stanley was on good terms with all his neighbors and acquaintances, whether they were Filipino, Japanese, Polynesian, or black. He spent hours with black friends, playing poker and bridge or just chatting. But Barry was sure that his grandfather didn't really understand these other men, and that he wasn't as close to them as he assumed.

Brooding about all these things, Barry was confused about what conclusions to draw. He believed that his white friends sincerely liked him, and he knew that his white grandparents loved him dearly. But none of them would ever understand what it was like to be black.

In spite of his inner turmoil, Barry was well liked at Punahou, and most of his friends were white. They never suspected that Barry had any problems. In the afternoons after school, they would often hang out at his grand-parents' apartment. It wasn't too far from the school, and Stanley Dunham welcomed the boys' company. They liked Stanley, too.

One reason Barry liked basketball so much was that some of the best professional basketball players were black. Julius "Dr. J" Erving, the star player for the Philadelphia 76ers at the time, was an athlete of exciting grace and style—a magnetic role model. Barry also loved the way he and the other boys could get completely caught up in playing a game. Then it didn't seem to matter what color anyone's skin was or how much money his family had. On the basketball court, at least, Barry felt like he belonged. He was especially good at long jump shots, and his team-mates called him "Barry O'Bomber."

While Barry didn't regret staying in Hawaii, he often felt lonely. His mother wrote him loving letters from Indonesia, and he knew she was thinking about him and making plans for his future. But he longed for a mother and father at home. He didn't share these feelings with his classmates, but he talked more freely with an older boy, Keith Kakugawa, also of mixed race.

Meanwhile, through her letters Ann urged her son to keep his grade point average up and think about college. Although Barry generally made Bs, in his last year or so he let his studies slide. His grandparents worried that he might even do something that would land him in jail, but they didn't confront him about his behavior.

At the beginning of Barry's senior year in high school, his mother returned to Hawaii for a while. She was alarmed by Barry's sinking grades, and by the serious trouble that some of his friends had gotten into. She gave Barry a talking-to: It was time for him to give up his lazy frame of mind and break away from the easy life in Hawaii. In order to do something worthwhile with his life, he should aim to go to a good college on the mainland after graduation.

Barry had been thinking that he'd rather take classes in Honolulu, work part-time, and coast along. He argued back, but in the end, his mother made him feel guilty. Pulling himself together, Barry applied to several colleges on the mainland. He won a full scholarship to Occidental College, a small liberal arts school in Los Angeles, and he decided to go there.

In the spring of 1979, Barry graduated from high school. His mother and Maya flew to Hawaii from Indonesia for the ceremony. In his personal section of the Punahou year-book, Barry thanked his grandmother and grandfather. Barry was a normal self-absorbed teenager in some ways, but he'd come to realize how much he owed Toot and Gramps.

The Dunhams had lived in a modest apartment in order to pay the difference between Barry's scholarship and his tuition fees. They'd shared their home with him, putting up with his adolescent sulkiness and thoughtless-ness. They'd worried about him day in and day out, as much as if they were his parents. A photo taken on gradua-tion day shows Stanley and Madelyn hugging Barry and beaming with pride.

CHAPTER 5

ON THE MAINLAND

LOS ANGELES IN 1979 WAS A LOOSE, SPRAWLING city of almost three million. Unlike Hawaii, it had a sizeable population of African-Americans—about one-tenth of the population of the city. Although the U.S. Civil Rights Act of 1968 had outlawed segregation in housing, most blacks lived in a few sections of the city such as Watts, East Los Angeles, and South Central.

These inner-city communities had long been plagued with unemployment, substandard schools, and crime. The residents felt that the city government did not respect them or serve them well, and they especially hated and mistrusted the Los Angeles Police Department. Simmering resentments sometimes broke out in violence, the worst being the Watts Riots of 1965.

However, Occidental College was located in Eagle

Rock, a quiet and well-to-do suburb of Los Angeles. The campus streets were lined with eucalyptus trees; the buildings were Spanish-style with red tile roofs. The other black students at Occidental, a small percentage of the student body, were mostly middle class, like Barry.

These students had various points of view on what it meant to be African-American. Some of them imitated the street talk of the black ghetto and spouted militant slogans. Others were determined to ignore racial tensions and live their own lives. "They weren't defined by the color of their skin, they would tell you," Obama wrote later in his autobiography. "They were individuals."

But Barry, still searching for a community where he belonged, couldn't ignore his background. He joined the Black Students' Association at Occidental. He started calling himself by his real name, his African father's name: Barack.

Unlike his mother and father, Barack had never been especially interested in politics. But at Occidental, he began to get involved. There was growing concern at Occidental and at other colleges across the United States about South Africa's policy of apartheid, or legal segregation by race.

At that time, South Africa was ruled by the white

minority descended from Dutch and British colonists. The blacks in South Africa were by far the majority of the population, but they lived in poverty. By law they could not vote in national elections or own land outside their "homelands," areas similar to the reservations for Native Americans in the United States. Although South Africa as a nation was prosperous, most of the wealth was owned and controlled by whites.

The United Nations had condemned apartheid for many years, but the United States and western European nations had hung back from breaking economic ties with South Africa over this issue. South Africa was an important trading partner for the United States, exporting diamonds, gold, and farm products, and importing machinery and other technology. Ronald Reagan, elected U.S. president in 1980, opposed any attempt to force South Africa to give up apartheid.

The organized resistance to apartheid in South Africa was the African National Congress (ANC), labeled a terrorist group by the U.S. State Department. The best-known leader of the ANC was Nelson Mandela, who had been in prison since 1964. The speech he gave when he was sentenced, "I Am Prepared to Die," was a source of inspiration for oppressed people all over the world. It also inspired Barack and many other college students.

Barack and his activist friends joined the movement to urge Americans to oppose the injustice in South Africa. One tactic was divestment, or refusing to own stock in South African businesses or in U.S. companies who did business in South Africa. Many colleges, including Occidental, owned investments in South Africa, and students began to demonstrate to get the trustees of the college to sell those tainted investments.

At a divestment rally on the Occidental campus, Barack discovered that he had a talent for public speaking. When he got up to talk about apartheid, an issue that could really change many people's lives, he spoke from the heart. He realized that he could make a crowd pay attention to what he was saying. That incident gave him an inkling that he could find his identity by reaching beyond himself, using his intelligence and talents to help other people.

During his two years at Occidental, Barack began to turn his attention away from his own individual search for identity. He was inspired by the example of Nelson Mandela, the imprisoned leader of the ANC in South Africa. He realized that it might be more satisfying to search for his mission in life. What could he do for other people? This had always been his mother's attitude, which she'd tried to pass on to him. Now it began to sink in.

Gradually, Barack spent less of his time partying and playing basketball. He decided not to try out for the school basketball team, because it would take up too much of his time. He still played basketball, but just pickup games for fun and exercise. He didn't necessarily study any harder, but professors were impressed with his intelligence and ability to express his thoughts. There were plenty of other thinkers, students and faculty, to argue with at Occidental, and Barack discovered that he enjoyed debating and was good at it.

One particular instructor at Occidental, political scientist Roger Boesche, urged Barack to study harder and make use of his talents. His course Modern Political Thought was Barack's favorite during his time at Occidental College. But Barack was angry when Boesche gave him a B on one exam, because he knew his actual score was as high as some students who'd received As.

When Barack questioned his grade, his instructor simply said, "You didn't apply yourself." Like Barack's mother, Boesche wanted him to work up to his potential, not just to do well without really trying. The message was that it wasn't all right to just coast on his talents—he had a responsibility to use them well.

The atmosphere in Los Angeles was more mentally challenging for Barack than it had been in easygoing Hawaii. Madelyn Dunham noticed that her grandson became more purposeful about his life during his two years there. He actually told her that he wanted "to leave the world a better place." Maya, who was following in his footsteps at Punahou School, also noticed a new thoughtfulness and sense of focus about her brother.

Barack was attracted to the field of public policy, the study of governmental decisions that can change the circumstances of people's everyday lives. U.S. policy of trading with South Africa, in spite of that country's policy of legal segregation, was a good example of such decisions. Barack was also pulled in the direction of becoming a writer.

By the spring of 1981, Barack felt he was ready for a bigger challenge than Occidental College. He decided to transfer to Columbia University in New York for his last two years of college. While Occidental was an excellent college, it was small. Columbia was a world-renowned university with a diverse student body. Columbia had produced numerous Nobel Prize winners; it was the home of the prestigious Pulitzer Prize for journalism. In the field of public policy, the faculty at Columbia included such names as Zbigniew Brzezinski, former national security adviser to President Jimmy Carter, and Zalmay Khalilzad, who would serve in several presidents' administrations and eventually become the U.S. ambassador to the United Nations.

One of the strongest attractions of Columbia for Barack was its location: New York, one of the great cities of the world, rather than sprawling, decentralized Los Angeles. Also, a predominantly black section of New York, Harlem, was famous as a center for black music, literature, and politics. Malcolm X had once thrilled African-American audiences with his oratory in Harlem. Musicians Barack loved, like Billie Holiday, had flourished in Harlem. African-American writers he admired, including Langston Hughes and Richard Wright, had lived and worked in Harlem. Harlem, Barack felt, might be the place where he would find his African-American community.

CHAPTER 6
NEW YORK CITY

IN AUGUST 1981 BARACK OBAMA ARRIVED IN NEW York. His goal of finding his place in an African-American community seemed reasonable at first, since the Columbia University campus was in uptown Manhattan, at the edge of Harlem. As a transfer student, Barack would live off campus rather than in a dormitory, so he intended to find an apartment in Harlem. But all the available apartments in Harlem were either in an exclusive district, much too expensive for a scholarship student, or in slums.

The biggest divide in New York, Barack found, wasn't between white and black so much as between rich and poor. On the one hand, there was the New York City of skyscrapers, power, and fabulous wealth. On the other hand, there was the New York City of the underprivileged, the hopelessly poor, and the crime-ridden neighborhoods.

Barack managed to find a low-rent apartment not too far from Columbia, but he failed to find a community. Instead, he fell into a solitary way of life, studying and reading on his own. He spent most of his spare time with challenging books such as the Bible, the novels of Herman Melville and Toni Morrison, and the philosophy of Friedrich Nietzsche. While Barack exercised his mind vigorously, he also went for long runs up and down Manhattan to exercise his body. Throughout high school Barack had been big as well as tall, but during his college years he gradually grew leaner and leaner.

Thinking ahead two years to his graduation from college, Barack planned to travel to Kenya and finally see his father again. The idea had come to him while he was still in Los Angeles. Back in high school, he'd stopped writing to his father, and after a while his father had stopped writing to him. But now Barack felt a need to get in touch with his father.

Before Barack left Occidental, he wrote to Barack Sr. and told him that he wanted to visit Kenya after he graduated from college. His father wrote back, telling him it was important for him to meet the African side of his family, "and also that you know where you belong." Where he belonged was exactly what Barack wanted to know most. However, it didn't occur to him that his father also needed to see him. Barack imagined Barack Sr. as a wealthy, important man with a happy family life in Kenya.

The summer after Barack's first year at Columbia, his mother and Maya came to New York to visit. They found him in his shabby apartment surrounded by piles of serious books, and not much else. Barack criticized his sister for reading *People*, a magazine of light articles about the lives of celebrities. Evidently he didn't remember how his father had criticized him, at age ten, for wanting to watch *How the Grinch Stole Christmas!* instead of studying.

Hearing that Barack was planning to visit his father after graduation, his mother talked to him at length about her first husband. She didn't want Barack to feel resentful toward his father, to blame him for leaving their family. She explained that she was the one who had divorced Barack Sr. When he visited them in Hawaii when Barack was ten, he had asked her to come to Kenya with him, but she had refused.

Listening to his mother, Barack was moved that she cared so deeply for his father. She obviously wanted the best for him, even after the sad failure of their marriage.

. . .

At Columbia, Barack majored in political science, with an emphasis on international relations. He was studying hard for the first time. The course work and the professors were more challenging at Columbia than at Occidental, and the other students were more competitive and ambitious. Barack became practiced and confident in debating.

During his senior year Barack took a seminar, a class with only eight students, on foreign policy. The focus of the class was on the uses of foreign aid and how wealth flowed between first-world countries, like the United States, and third-world countries, like Kenya. For his senior thesis, Barack chose the topic of Soviet nuclear disarmament. Ever since the end of World War II, the United States and the Soviet Union (controlled by Russia) had been locked in an arms race. Nuclear war and other harm from nuclear weapons had been a constant threat.

President Jimmy Carter had made some progress in negotiating the Strategic Arms Limitation Treaty with the Soviet Union in 1979. But President Ronald Reagan urged a massive arms buildup. These two different choices in foreign policy could have serious consequences for not only the United States and Russia but also the entire world.

During Barack's last year at Columbia, several months before graduation, his phone rang one morning as he was fixing breakfast. It was his aunt Jane, his father's sister, calling from Nairobi, Kenya. Barack Obama Sr. had been killed in a car accident. Aunt Jane asked him to call his uncle Roy, who was living in Boston, and let him know.

Barack was so stunned that he didn't know what he felt. All these years he had heard stories about his father, wondered about him, gazed at pictures of him, and been urged to become a noble person like him. Now Barack would not be able to see him to find out what he was really like.

With Barack's father gone, it didn't seem so urgent to go to Kenya, and he put off the trip. He sent condolences to his father's family, though, and asked them to write. His half sister Auma, who had been born in Kenya shortly before Barack was born in Hawaii, was startled to see how much Barack's handwriting looked like their father's.

Auma was Barack Sr.'s second child. Auma's mother, Kezia, was Barack's village wife. Kezia had been pregnant with Auma when Barack Sr. left Kenya to study at the University of Hawaii. Now Auma wrote back to Barack, and they began a correspondence.

. . .

At Columbia, Barack had decided that he wanted to become a community organizer. He didn't know anyone who had that kind of job. He didn't know exactly what a community organizer would do, except that somehow he would help poor black people take control of their lives.

Barack was inspired by the civil rights movement of the late 1950s and early 1960s. He knew that in spite of progress made by Dr. Martin Luther King Jr. and others, there was still a lot to be done. He believed that if people in poor neighborhoods worked together, they could better their lives, and he wanted to be part of the process. It seemed like a way for him to belong to a community, a community of people who were cooperating to bring about justice. He longed for that.

Barack also knew that community organizers weren't well paid, so first he needed to pay off his student loans and save some money. After graduating from Columbia in 1983 with high honors, Barack got a job at the Business International Corporation. This small company published newsletters on international finance and consulted for U.S. firms doing business outside the country. Barack worked as a research assistant and edited a yearbook, *Financing Foreign*

Operations. Barack learned a great deal about the business world and international finance.

Barack's work at Business International Corporation was well paid, so he could afford an apartment in a better neighborhood, on the Upper East Side of Manhattan. Wearing a suit and tie and carrying a briefcase to work, using the services of a secretary pool, Barack felt like a different person—and it wasn't the person he'd planned to be. He was more aware than ever of the sharp divide between rich and poor in New York, and he was afraid that if he went over to the rich side, he'd end up with the wrong values.

However, the other black employees—the secretaries and the security guard for the building—urged him to keep on this track toward more money, more power. They told him his ideals of helping poor people were naïve and foolish. And sometimes he wondered if they were right.

One day while Barack was working on the computer at Business International, he received a call from his African half sister, who was studying in Germany. Barack and Auma had been writing off and on since their father's death. Now she was planning to come to the United States for a visit, and she wanted to see him.

Barack was excited and happy—until she called again with bad news. Their half brother David, the younger son of their father's third wife, had been killed in a motorcycle accident. So the news was doubly bad: a half brother whom Barack had never seen was dead, and he and Auma would not be able to meet, at least not for now. Instead of coming to New York, she had to fly to Kenya for David's funeral.

A few months later Barack resigned from the consulting firm and started looking for a job as a community organizer. Although he sent out dozens of résumés, no one seemed to want to hire him. He took a job for a few months with New York Public Interest Research Group, an organization inspired by political activist Ralph Nader. They sent him to City College of New York (CCNY) to work with minority students, but he didn't feel that he was accomplishing much there.

During this period, in 1984, Barack got his first glimpse of the White House. He and student leaders from CCNY traveled to Washington, D.C., to deliver a petition to the senators and congressmen representing New York. The petition protested President Ronald Reagan's proposal to cut student aid, which would hurt many of the low–income college students in Harlem.

On this first trip to Washington, Barack had just enough time to visit the National Mall and gaze down the length of the Reflecting Pool from the Washington Monument to the Lincoln Memorial. He also made a point of taking a look at the White House from Pennsylvania Avenue. He was impressed that ordinary citizens could get so close to the president's residence, in spite of the fact that President Reagan had been shot and almost killed by an assassin at the beginning of his term. Barack thought that the openness expressed Americans' confidence in their democracy.

Back in New York, Barack continued to search for a job in his chosen field, but he was out of money. Just as he was thinking of going back to work in the business world, he got a call from Jerry Kellman, a community organizer in Chicago. Kellman himself was white and Jewish. He was looking for a person of color to work in Chicago's poor black neighborhoods, where white people were automatically distrusted.

When Kellman and Barack met for an interview, Kellman was delighted to find a college-educated black man who wanted the low-paying job. Barack, for his part, was eager to pursue his goal of serving society. He left for Chicago in June 1985.

When Ann heard about Barack's new job, she was happy for her son. Although she was on the other side of the world, she felt connected to him because the purpose of their work was similar. By getting to know the poor women in Indonesian villages, she'd learned that acquiring a loom, a sewing machine, or a cow could transform them into self-sufficient small business owners. Years earlier, when Ann was a young woman and Barry was a young boy in Indonesia, they'd shared the frustration of wanting to help people in need but not knowing how. Now they had each found a practical approach.

CHAPTER 7
COMMUNITY ORGANIZER

BARACK OBAMA HAD SEEN CHICAGO ONLY ONCE before, on his trip to the mainland with Toot and his mother, the summer he turned eleven. But he'd heard a lot about the lives of African-American people in Chicago. A friend from Occidental College had grown up in a close-knit neighborhood on the South Side. And one of his grandfather's friends in Honolulu was a poet who'd lived in Chicago during the Great Depression and the 1940s. Barack had also read Richard Wright's autobiography, *Black Boy*, about his life in Chicago as a young man.

In the first half of the twentieth century, millions of black people had migrated to the North, hoping for better jobs and for relief from the legal segregation and violence of the South. Chicago was a major destination of these migrants, and in the 1980s it held the largest group of African–Americans of any U.S. city. As Barack knew, Chicago also had a reputation as the most segregated city in America.

The mid–1980s were a hopeful but also frustrating time for the black population of Chicago. Two years before Barack arrived in Chicago, Harold Washington had been elected the city's first African–American mayor. Mayor Washington wanted to institute a progressive program to reform Chicago politics and improve the lives of the poor black population. However, he was fiercely opposed by a majority of the city council.

To add to the tension, many working–class people, white and black, had lost their jobs in the preceding few years. South Chicago used to be a center of heavy industry, but in the early 1980s, Wisconsin Steel, U.S. Steel, and other large manufacturing plants had closed. There were no other well-paying jobs for blue-collar workers to replace the ones that vanished. Driving around Chicago, Barack saw for himself the huge empty, rusting factories.

Jerry Kellman had Barack start working in Roseland, a neighborhood on the Far South Side of Chicago. This part of the city was almost all black, although not all poor. There were blocks of middle-class homes among the blocks of rundown apartment buildings with extremely poor tenants.

A public housing project named Altgeld Gardens was Barack's first assignment. The very location of Altgeld Gardens was depressing. On one side was the polluted Calumet River; on another, the Lake Calumet landfill, one of the largest dumps in the country. Also close by was the city's sewage treatment plant, and its smell was always heavy in the air.

About two thousand people, almost all of them black, lived in Altgeld Gardens. The two-story brick apartment buildings, originally built for industrial workers, were now forty years old. The Chicago Housing Authority (CHA) was supposed to make repairs to crumbling ceilings or broken toilets and heaters, but it might take them months to do the work. Sometimes they didn't show up at all.

Kellman advised Barack to start by meeting with the residents and talking with them. He should listen carefully to learn what changes might make a real difference in their lives. Then he was to help them organize to achieve the change. The idea was for the people in the community to take action for themselves, changing their conviction that nothing could be done. Positive action would give them confidence in their own power, and confidence would then enable them to make other positive changes.

Barack began working out of a little office in a local church, calling dozens of residents to set up interviews. Listening to story after discouraging story, he began to get the big picture. Twenty years earlier, civil rights laws had ended racial discrimination in housing and employment. Many African-Americans had then been able to get better jobs and to move their families from crowded parts of the city to homes in Roseland. But whites promptly moved out of these neighborhoods, and property values fell.

After dozens of interviews, Barack concluded that what the people in the Altgeld community cared about most was jobs. Unemployment ran high, especially among young men. Many of them turned to gangs and crime, making the streets unsafe for ordinary citizens.

The volunteer workers grew fond of Barack. They called him "Baby Face" because he was so young, idealistic, and naïve. They watched him discover what they already knew: No one at city hall cared what happened at Altgeld Gardens.

Barack's first bright idea was to work through the black churches in the area. The black churches in Chicago were powerful social forces, and if only they would work together, they could bring about changes that would help all of their people. But one of the South Side pastors, the Reverend Jeremiah A. Wright Jr., explained to Barack that his bright idea didn't fit reality. The churches, fiercely independent and suspicious of one another, would be impossible to organize.

Barack soon realized the truth of what Wright said. To each pastor, particularly ones with large followings, organizing with other churches meant sharing some of their power. Furthermore, the black pastors were suspicious of Barack—a young man from New York in the pay of white people—trying to tell the pastors what to do.

After months of hard work characterized by failure and frustration, Barack finally enjoyed a small success. The Chicago city government had an employment department, the Mayor's Office of Employment and Training (MET). But there was no job intake and training center on the Far South Side, where the jobs were most desperately needed. Barack arranged a meeting between the director of MET and the residents of Altgeld and the neighborhood involved in the issue.

By the time the meeting was over, the director had agreed to put an MET center in the area. Barack felt deeply gratified, not just for his own success but also for that of the community residents. They had organized, they had taken action, and they had gotten results.

One thing that impressed Barack about the volunteers working with him in discouraging conditions was how many of them drew on their faith for strength. Barack had not been brought up in a religious tradition. Toot and Gramps were both from Christian backgrounds, but they didn't attend church. His mother was respectful of all religions, but she didn't have a faith in any one of them. Barack's father (whom he'd hardly known, anyway) was an atheist. His stepfather, Lolo, was Muslim but didn't practice his faith seriously.

Until Barack came to Chicago, he'd followed his mother's lead of respecting all religions—from a distance. Ann Dunham seemed to be one of those rare people who was deeply spiritual and ethical, but felt no personal connection to an organized religion. That worked for her, and until now Barack hadn't felt a need for religion, either. But now, struggling to serve in the African–American community, he realized that he also needed the strength of a faith community. He began dropping in at various churches on Sunday mornings, and he talked to several pastors about his doubts and hopes.

63

The religious community where Barack seemed to fit in best was Trinity United Church of Christ, a large church in the Hyde Park neighborhood on the South Side of Chicago. The pastor, Jeremiah Wright, was a preacher of personal magnetism who had built his congregation from only ninety members to several thousand. More important to Barack, Wright and his church were committed to the social justice element of Christian belief. Barack had noticed Trinity in the first place because he saw a sign on its lawn protesting apartheid in South Africa.

Also, Wright was an educated, intelligent man, willing to have long discussions with Barack about faith and how it related to the problems of poverty, racism, and injustice. Sitting in the congregation on Sundays, Barack wasn't sure what he believed, but he wanted to be part of this church.

One particular sermon of Wright's, titled "The Audacity of Hope," struck him especially. The pastor spoke forcefully about all the injustice and violence and suffering in the world in general, and the sorrows of this congregation in particular. But then he talked even more forcefully about the hope that keeps people going and allows them to praise God in spite of everything. Everyone in the church was moved, and Barack had tears in his eyes.

. . .

During Barack's years as a community organizer in Chicago, his Kenyan half sister, Auma, came to meet him at last. She was living in Germany now, where she'd gone to study after she graduated from high school. To the delight and relief of both of them, they felt close and comfortable with each other from their first hug at the Chicago airport.

Barack showed his sister his little office in the church in Roseland and introduced her to the volunteers who worked with him. Auma told Barack many things about their father, whom she called "the Old Man."

Barack knew part of the story: Barack Obama Sr. had returned to Kenya in 1965 with a master's degree in economics from Harvard. He got a good job with an American petroleum company, and then he gained appointments in the Kenyan government. Barack had the impression from his father's letters that the Old Man had been a respected and important man in Kenya all his life.

But Auma explained that Kenya, independent from Great Britain for only a few decades, was split over tribal loyalties. The largest tribe in Kenya was the Kikuyus, and the Old Man felt that Jomo Kenyatta favored Kikuyus over the Luo, the Obama family's tribe. The Old Man saw other men promoted over him just because they were Kikuyu. When the Old Man complained, he lost his position in the Kenyan Ministry of Finance.

Meanwhile, the Old Man had brought Auma, four years old, and her older brother, Roy, six, to live with him and his new American wife, Ruth Nidesand, in Nairobi. Ruth and the Old Man eventually had two boys, Mark and David. At first the family was very well-off, with a big house to live in and a Mercedes to drive.

But after the Old Man fell out of favor with the government, he couldn't get another job. No one, not even American companies, would hire an enemy of Kenyatta's. The Old Man drank heavily, and he grew bitter and quarrelsome. Ruth left him, taking Mark and David.

The Old Man became so poor that he and his two oldest children hardly had enough to eat. Roy left home to live with relatives until he finished his education at the University of Nairobi. Auma loyally stuck with her father until she was old enough to escape to Germany to finish her own education. The Old Man suffered a series of car accidents, and finally he died in one.

Listening to Auma's stories, Barack was dazed. In his letters, his father had said nothing about all this. All those years when they were writing back and forth, Barack had imagined his father riding around Kenya in a Mercedes, conferring with top officials. Barack Obama Sr., in Barack's imagination, had been an exalted role model for his American son. Now Barack realized that his father, although a brilliant man with high ideals, had also been a human being with flaws.

At the end of Auma's stay in Chicago, she and Barack agreed to meet in Kenya some day soon and visit their African family together. Then Auma left, and Barack flew to Washington, D.C., where their older brother, Roy, now lived. Roy added his view to Auma's description of their father: a man with three different families, unable to be a responsible father to any of his children.

Talking with Auma and Roy and watching the African-American families on the South Side of Chicago, Barack thought about how different his own life might have been. If he'd lived in Kenya, he might have been like Roy, growing up with a father who was unemployed, angry, and often drunk. Or if Barack had lived in Altgeld Gardens, he might have been like one of the young men he saw hanging around street corners, acting cool and tough, dying at an early age or ending up in prison.

Instead, Barack had always had a secure home with his mother and his grandparents. He had enjoyed an excellent education and a range of job opportunities. He was lucky. More than ever, he was determined to do something for others, to share his good luck.

As a community organizer, one of Barack's biggest successes was a campaign to get the asbestos removed from the apartments in Altgeld Gardens. The Chicago Housing Authority didn't want residents even to know about the asbestos and its dangers, and the residents found out about it only accidentally. With Barack's help, a group of residents confronted the housing authority and demanded the asbestos be removed.

However, as time went on, Barack began to think that community organizing was not the best way for him to make a difference in people's lives. While he could work for months without making any headway at all, the mayor of Chicago could create big changes in schools, neighborhoods, or families just by giving an order. Also, Harold Washington had an important effect on people's lives just because he was a public leader they felt connected to.

Barack could see that this politician was the focus for

the hopes and dreams of thousands of people. He noticed Washington's picture on the wall in African-American homes and places of business all over southern Chicago. When Mayor Washington died suddenly of a heart attack in November 1987, the black community was grief stricken. They were deprived of a leader who had brought them together and given them pride.

Maybe, Barack thought, the way to make big changes was to get into politics. And the way to get into politics was to earn a law degree. The U.S. government was a system of self-government by laws, and so was the government of Illinois and of the city of Chicago. Politicians like congressmen and senators made laws. Politicians like presidents, governors, and mayors applied the laws. If you knew the laws, you could make them work for the people you represented.

That's how Harold Washington had started, by studying law. So had Abraham Lincoln, for that matter.

CHAPTER 8
KENYA

IN MAY 1988 BARACK QUIT HIS COMMUNITY ORGA-
nizer job in Chicago. He'd been accepted at Harvard Law
School for that fall, and now he was going to spend the
summer traveling. First he toured Europe for three weeks,
and then he flew from London to Kenya. He would stay in
Kenya for five weeks, getting to know the African side of
his family. He hoped that Kenya would help him to better
understand his father.

Auma was now teaching at the University of Nairobi,
and she picked Barack up at Jomo Kenyatta International
Airport. In Nairobi, Barack met his father's sisters, includ–
ing Aunt Jane, who had called him six years earlier with
the news of his father's death. He met Kezia, Obama Sr.'s
first wife and Auma and Roy's mother; his half brother
Bernard, Kezia's youngest son; and many other aunts,

uncles, and cousins. Bernard's older brother Abo was living on the family farm in Kogelo, so Barack would not meet him until later.

The African Obamas welcomed Barack as long-lost family, whether they were actually related to him by blood or not. They all called him "Barry"; that was the name that Barack Obama Sr. had always used when he talked about his American son. Barack realized that his father had talked about him often, with pride.

Barack's half brother Roy joined the gathering, flying into Nairobi from Washington, D.C. The family celebrated with a feast, including typical Kenyan foods like *chapos* (flat bread), *sukuma wiki* (collard greens), and *ugali* (cornmeal cake).

It was a new feeling for Barack, to be embraced by a huge extended family. It was also a new feeling for him to be in a city—a country, nearly a whole continent— full of people who looked like him. In the U.S., the first thing most people noticed about him was that his skin was darker than theirs. Here, people wanted to know first which tribe he belonged to.

Although Barack's father had been dead for several years, Barack almost felt that he was present with him in

Nairobi. As he walked the same streets where his father had walked, and talked to the people who had known him, he understood Kenya better, and he understood better what his father's life here had been like.

Barack had seen poverty in Indonesia, New York, and Chicago. But he'd never seen such a concentration of poverty as in Nairobi. One large section on the outskirts of the city was a vast shantytown called Kibera, Africa's worst slum.

Kibera spread across a valley, acre after acre of cardboard and plywood shacks along dirt paths, with open sewers and no clean water. Since the people had no legal right to be there, Nairobi didn't provide any services. Some 500,000 people lived there, and often ten people lived in a one-room hut.

Barack made a special trip to Kibera to meet his aunt Sarah—Barack Sr.'s older sister. Sarah and Barack Sr.'s mother, Akumu, was their father Onyango's first wife. But Akumu had been unhappy in the Obama family and left them early on. Barack Sr. had actually been raised by his father's second wife, also named Sarah but called "Granny" by everyone. Recently, Aunt Sarah had quarreled with the rest of the family over the Old Man's inheritance.

There were other family quarrels. Ruth—Barack Sr.'s

second American wife—had divorced Barack Sr. and separated herself and her two sons from the rest of the family. It was her younger son, David, who had died in a motorcycle accident a few years earlier. She still lived in Nairobi, and she and her older son, Mark, a student at Stanford University in California, now wanted to meet Barack.

Ruth and Mark showed Barack family pictures from the years that Auma and Roy had lived with Ruth, the Old Man, and their children, Mark and David. Barack thought about how different his life might have been if his mother, Ann, had taken him to live with his father in Kenya. Again he considered how lucky he was.

Barack also puzzled over the tangled relationships in the families his father had come from and the families his father had created. The wonderful thing about an African family was that family members were so loyal to one another. Families expected to care for all their members, even a half brother like Barack who had grown up in America.

But family ties could also be burdensome. Auma felt that their father had been dragged down by all the people he felt responsible for—not only his wives and children but all his relatives, all his tribespeople, all of the many people who expected something of him.

Barack could understand that, because he found himself worrying about his young half brother Bernard. At seventeen, Bernard was easygoing and agreeable, but he was even more aimless than Barack had been at the same age. When Barack tried to talk to him about plans for the future, he felt that Bernard seemed to have no ambition at all.

During Barack's second week in Kenya, he and Auma left Nairobi to go on a safari in the Great Rift Valley. It was only a day's trip by van from the capital city to the valley. Barack was thrilled at the sight of the wide plains roamed by lions, giraffes, and hippos, and by great herds of zebras and wildebeests. He was awestruck to think that, according to paleontologists, human beings originated on this very part of the planet.

The heart of Barack's Kenya stay, though, was his visit to the farm, near the village of Kolego in Luo country, where his father had grown up. When Auma visited Barack in Chicago, she had described the family homestead in loving detail: the tree-shaded compound with the cow and the chickens, the smell of smoke from the wood fire, Granny telling amusing stories.

Auma and Roy had spent much of their childhood in Nairobi, but Auma's happiest memories were of the compound in Kolego. "Home Squared," Auma and Roy called it. Your Home Squared was the place your ancestors came from, your true home.

Barack, Auma, and Roy, as well as several other family members, traveled to the farm. First they took a train overnight to the city of Kisumu, near the western shore of Lake Victoria. Then they rode a bus for several hours. The bus was so crowded that Barack had to sit with chickens on his lap.

Getting off at the gold-mining town of Ndori, Barack and the others took a jitney van into the hills. Here, at the farm where the Old Man had been raised, two more uncles met the travelers. Later Barack would also meet his half brother Abo. The uncles led the visitors through the tall hedges that enclosed the family compound, Home Squared.

Besides several small round huts, the compound contained the square main house with concrete walls and a corrugated iron roof, draped with flowering vines. Granny, the woman who had raised Barack Obama Sr. as her own son, came out to greet them. With a hug, she welcomed Barack as her grandson.

Granny couldn't speak English and Barack couldn't

speak the Luo language, but they smiled at each other. They sat down under a mango tree in the center of the compound, and she told him the story of his family. Auma translated, sitting with Barack and their grandmother, as Granny braided her hair. Granny's story started several generations prior, describing the lives and customs of the Obamas before Europeans arrived in Kisumu.

In the course of the story Granny told Barack a great deal about his grandfather, her husband, Hussein Onyango Obama. Barack had imagined him as an independent, proud Kenyan nationalist. After all, he was the man who had written Ann Dunham's parents that he didn't want his son marrying a white woman.

But actually Onyango had worked for many years as a servant to various white men. Granny still had Onyango's official papers from that time, when the British ruled Kenya, a passbook identifying him as a domestic servant. However, Onyango had not remained a servant. Learning modern farming techniques, he had developed the land that the family now lived on. He had turned a tract of unproductive bush into a self-sustaining farm.

Barack's grandfather and father were both buried behind the house, near a cornfield. Their graves were two cement slabs side by side. Barack sat between the graves and shed tears, and he finally felt that he'd found the connection he'd been looking for all his life.

During their stay in Kolego, Auma took a picture of Barack sitting beside Granny. In the photo, both of them are smiling happily. He is leaning toward her, while she strokes his hair with one hand.

CHAPTER 9

LAW SCHOOL AND MICHELLE

ENTERING HARVARD LAW SCHOOL IN SEPTEMBER 1988, Barack Obama was twenty-seven. He was older than most of his classmates, and his experience was broader. Although he hadn't accomplished nearly as much as he'd wanted to as a community organizer, he had learned a great deal from his years in Chicago. His trip to Kenya, too, had helped him sort out how he intended to use his life. He now had a clearer idea of his goals, and he had the discipline to achieve them.

Barack spent most of his three years of law school in the library, reading, studying, and writing. Researching legal cases and statutes was often tedious, and sometimes the legal arguments were over petty details. Barack saw, also, that laws could be used by people with power merely as a way to control the people without power. However, the main result of his studies was to deepen his respect for the law, especially the constitution, the undergirding of the U.S. legal system. Later, he described American law as the record of "a long-running conversation, a nation arguing with its conscience."

While Barack studied the law, he also worked as a research aide for a professor, the famous legal scholar Laurence Tribe. This was valuable experience, because Tribe was one of the foremost liberal constitutional law experts in the country. He frequently presented cases before the U.S. Supreme Court. Tribe later remembered Barack Obama as his "most amazing research assistant."

At the end of his first year of law school, Barack was selected as one of the seventy student editors of the *Harvard Law Review.* This was an honor, because the editors were selected on the basis of their first-year grades and their entry in a writing competition, as well as recommendations from instructors and other students.

The early 1990s was a period of racial discord at Harvard. A group of black students confronted the university, asking for more minority representation on the faculty. Derrick Bell, an African-American and a tenured professor at Harvard Law School, resigned his position in 1992 in protest over the lack of women of color among the faculty. Barack was deeply impressed with Bell's action, and he gave a speech praising Bell and calling for a more representative faculty; otherwise, he was not much involved in the disputes over racial issues.

Barack was active in the Black Law Students Association, but he made good friends among both black and white students. His focus for the most part was on combating injustice for poor people. At one meeting of the black students at Harvard's law, medical, and business schools, the topic of discussion was whether they wanted to call themselves "black" or "African-American." Barack's opinion was that it didn't matter very much. As his friend Cassandra Butts remembered it, he told the meeting, "You know, whether we're called black or African-Americans doesn't make a whole heck of a lot of difference to the lives of people who are working hard, you know, living day to day, in Chicago, in New York."

Barack took part in the antiapartheid movement on the Harvard campus. In the years since his Occidental College days, when he first realized what an important issue apartheid was, there had been some hopeful developments for South Africa. In 1986, Congress had passed the Comprehensive Anti-Apartheid Act over President Reagan's veto. This law banned all new U.S. trade and investment in South Africa. The law was to remain in effect until the white South African government eliminated apartheid and released ANC leader Nelson Mandela from prison.

At the end of his second year, in 1990, Barack was elected president of the *Harvard Law Review.* This was a great honor, and the competition was fierce. As the first African-American president of the *Harvard Law Review,* Barack made the national news after his election was announced in February.

Barack was chosen as president partly because of his high-quality work in his courses but also because he had a reputation for not taking sides in the bitter political and personal arguments that raged through the law school. Although Barack was politically liberal, conservatives respected him as a fair-minded thinker. He could see their point of view, even if he didn't agree with it. Since he had to manage the seventy strong-willed student editors, as well as all the other legal writers who wanted to be published in the *Harvard Law Review,* this fair-minded approach served him well. His policy as president was to allow a range of opinions to be expressed, to encourage the editors to work together, and to maintain the high quality of the journal.

While Barack Obama was progressing toward a law degree, his personal life changed dramatically. During the summer of 1989, after his first year of law school, he worked as a summer associate at the Chicago law firm of Sidley Austin. The attorney who was assigned to show him around the firm and help train him was the only African-American attorney in the office: Michelle Robinson.

Barack was smitten at first sight. Michelle, a tall, confident young woman with striking looks, was more skeptical of him—she could see that he was intelligent, ambitious, and charming, but she was looking for deeper qualities. Besides, she didn't think it was appropriate to date someone she worked with.

But Barack persisted, and Michelle warmed up to him. Their first date was to see Spike Lee's movie *Do the Right Thing*, about racial conflict in a multiethnic neighborhood in Brooklyn, New York. The more Michelle got to know Barack, the more impressed she was by his unusual background, his work as a community organizer, and his plans for the future. She realized that he was a deep-thinking person with high ideals.

As for Barack, he was almost as attracted to Michelle's family as he was to her. She'd grown up in a close-knit black community in Chicago. Her parents, Frasier and Marian Robinson, were also both from Chicago. The Robinsons had raised Michelle and her older brother, Craig, in a four-room bungalow on the South Side. Frasier worked as a city pump operator, in spite of being handicapped by multiple sclerosis, while Marian stayed home to raise the children.

Michelle's mother and father hadn't gone to college, and they were determined that their children would have the chance for a better education. They encouraged Michelle and Craig to work hard and respect their teachers, but also to think for themselves. Craig went to Princeton University on a basketball scholarship, and two years later Michelle also entered Princeton. After graduation from college, Michelle went on to Harvard Law School, graduating two years before Barack.

Barack admired the Robinsons, and he loved their stable, happy family life. While Barack was close with individual members of his family—for instance, he spent hours on the phone with his younger half sister, Maya—the family as a whole was fragmented and scattered over the globe.

The fact that Michelle's brother, Craig, was a former college basketball star was just icing on the cake to Barack. The two young men played pickup games together for fun, and Craig was impressed with Barack's confidence on the court. Craig was a much better player who could have made a career of professional basketball, but Barack was still eager to test his skills against Craig's.

During Barack's last two years at Harvard Law School, he and Michelle grew closer and closer. When Michelle's father died, Barack flew to Chicago to be with Michelle at the funeral.

In the spring of 1991, Barack graduated with high honors from Harvard Law School. He moved back to Chicago and passed the Illinois bar exam, required in order to practice law. There hadn't been much doubt that he would pass the exam, but he took Michelle out to dinner to celebrate. That night, he proposed marriage, and she accepted.

After they were engaged, Barack took Michelle to Hawaii and introduced her to his grandparents. Stanley Dunham was very taken with Michelle's good looks. Madelyn, always no-nonsense herself, cared more about whether her grandson's fiancée had a level head on her shoulders. She praised Michelle as "a very sensible girl."

Barack also took Michelle to Kenya so that she could meet the African side of his family. When they visited Granny in Kolego, the older Kenyan woman and the young American woman took to each other immediately. All the Obama relatives liked Michelle, in fact, and they were pleased that she quickly picked up a number of words and phrases in the Luo language.

Michelle had always wanted to visit Africa, the place her ancestors came from. However, from this trip she learned how American she was, and how glad she was to be American. Kenyans could be put in jail just for publishing criticisms of the government. Kenyans who wanted to start a business, or even get a job, had to bribe someone in power first.

For Barack, too, visiting Kenya again underscored his appreciation of his own country. From his years of studying law, he had a deeper understanding of the U.S. constitution and system of government. Barack saw, more than ever, that American democracy depended on equal opportunity and justice, and he was determined to work for these values.

Barack Obama and Michelle Robinson were married in October 1992. It was sad that Michelle's father hadn't lived to see this day. Barack's grandfather Stanley Dunham, too, died before the wedding.

Otherwise, the wedding was a joyous occasion. Jeremiah Wright, their pastor and by now a good friend, performed the ceremony at Trinity Church. Their family and friends gathered from around the country and from all over the world. Just on Barack's side of the guest list, Toot was there from Hawaii, Ann from Indonesia, Maya from New York, where she had just moved, Auma from Nairobi, and Roy from Washington, D.C., plus friends from Honolulu, Occidental College, New York, Chicago, and Harvard.

After the wedding, Barack and Michelle moved into a condominium in Hyde Park, a middle- to upper-class, racially mixed section of Chicago. Barack intended to join a law firm, but first he finished directing Illinois Project Vote, a program to register new voters in Chicago. It was an important election year, with President George H. W. Bush, Republican, running for reelection against Democrat Bill Clinton, governor of Arkansas.

Project Vote succeeded in registering almost 150,000 new voters, most of them black. That November, they helped elect Bill Clinton to the presidency. They also elected Carol Moseley Braun, a lawyer and Illinois state representative, the first African-American woman to become a U.S. senator.

In 1993, Barack joined the law firm of Davis, Miner, Barnhill & Galland in Chicago. They specialized in civil rights and discrimination cases. Barack, with his outstanding record at Harvard, was sought after by many law firms, and he could have made much more money practicing corporate law. But civil rights and discrimination cases were exactly the kind of work he wanted to do.

At the same time, Barack began working on a book. A publisher had already given him a contract and an advance for a book in 1991, when he made news as the first black president of the *Harvard Law Review*. In the fall of 1992, the University of Chicago, hoping to lure Obama as a permanent faculty member, offered him a fellowship and an office where he could work on the book.

Barack didn't set out to write a memoir, an account of his personal experiences. He intended his book to be an important analysis of race relations in the United States. He thought he'd finish it in one year. But the more he wrote, the more the book became his own personal story, and the more difficult it was to keep on schedule.

Through the writing, Barack explored his often con-fused and contradictory feelings about his background. He was the child of a white American mother and a black Kenyan father. He'd grown up in Hawaii and (for a few years) Indonesia, far from the mainland United States and Kenya. He'd experienced racial discrimination, but noth-ing like the oppressive segregation and prejudice that most black people in the United States were familiar with.

It was a lot to sort out, and it took Barack more than twice as long as he expected, even though he often stayed up late at night to work on the book. He wrote in a cramped room off the kitchen that Michelle called "The Hole." Michelle thought he was trying to accomplish too much at once, between a full-time job and an ambitious writing project.

Michelle Obama was a high achiever herself, at the time the founding director of the Chicago office of Pub-lic Allies. This public service program recruited, trained, and placed young people from diverse backgrounds in paid internships with nonprofit organizations. However, whatever her commitments, Michelle firmly believed in reserving time for a personal life with family and friends.

CHAPTER 10
INTO POLITICS

WHILE BARACK OBAMA WAS WRITING HIS BOOK, HE often consulted his mother to get the facts of his early life straight. Ann Dunham Sutoro (she had kept her second husband's last name, but changed the spelling) had lived in Indonesia for many years now. She had received a PhD from the University of Hawaii in anthropology. She worked energetically to better the condition of women in developing countries.

Ann had been one of the first to promote microcredit, or very small loans, to poor but enterprising women to help them start small businesses. With only enough money to buy a loom or a sewing machine, a woman could earn enough to lift herself and her family out of poverty and send her children to school. For such a small investment, microloans had an impressive effect for good. The idea caught on, and many governments as well as nonprofit organizations put it to use.

In 1994 Barack finished his book, which by now had turned into a full-fledged memoir titled *Dreams from My Father: A Story of Race and Inheritance.* The title fit the book well. Its major theme was Barack trying to connect with his missing father and his African background.

About the same time that *Dreams from My Father* came out, Ann discovered that she was seriously ill with cancer. She moved back to Hawaii, where her mother cared for her. Ann died at the age of fifty-two in November 1995, only a few months after Barack's book was published. Barack flew to Hawaii to be with his half sister Maya and his grandmother Madelyn. They scattered Ann Dunham Sutoro's ashes from cliffs overlooking the surf on the South Shore of Oahu.

Barack was sorry that he hadn't realized how close Ann was to death, and that he hadn't been with her when she died. He also regretted that he hadn't included more in *Dreams from My Father* about his mother, a remarkable woman who gave him his deepest values. "I know that she was the kindest, most generous spirit I have ever known," he wrote later in a preface to the 2004 edition of *Dreams*, "and that what is best in me I owe to her."

The first edition of *Dreams from My Father* received good reviews. The *New York Times Book Review* praised the way the book described "the phenomenon of belonging to two different worlds, and thus belonging to neither." The *Washington Post Book World* said, "Fluidly, calmly, insightfully, Obama guides us straight to the intersection of the most serious questions of identity, class, and race." However, *Dreams from My Father* sold less than 10,000 copies—not exactly a bestseller. The paperback edition sold even less, and the book went out of print.

But by now Barack was finished with writing about his past and was well into launching his political career. In 1995, when he was thirty-three, his first chance came up to run for an elected office. Alice Palmer, the state senator for the Thirteenth District, decided to run for Congress. That left her seat in the state legislature open.

Michelle was skeptical about a political career for her husband. She disliked politics, and she doubted that Barack would succeed—she thought he was too idealistic. But she supported him because he wanted so much to try and because she respected his goal of working for important reforms.

Barack started to put together a campaign. He would need an enthusiastic team of volunteers to work for his election, a network of influential people who would back his candidacy, and donors to fund the campaign. Judson Miner, a senior partner in the law firm where Barack worked, had been Mayor Washington's legal counsel, and Miner had many valuable contacts to share. Barack also had his own contacts from his successful direction of Project Vote in 1992. And Michelle, who had lived in Chicago all her life and had worked for Mayor Richard M. Daley as an aide, connected Barack with some influential people in the city.

A backer who raised about a tenth of the funds for Obama's campaign was Tony Rezko, a real estate developer. Obama was in favor of Chicago's policy to give developers tax credits for developing low-income sections of the city. With the tax credits, renovating run-down neighborhoods became an attractive business opportunity for developers like Rezko. And the city benefited from upgrading those sections.

When Obama announced his candidacy in September 1995, Alice Palmer herself endorsed him as her replacement. But a few months later, when it seemed that she would lose the Democratic primary for the U.S. House of Representatives, she decided to go for her old seat instead. She asked Barack Obama to bow out of the race at this point, but he refused. Now Palmer turned from his most important backer into his main opponent.

Alice Palmer would probably have won her state senate seat back, except that Obama's campaign challenged her nominating petitions. In order to get on the ballot, a candidate must have a certain number of registered voters sign his or her petitions. The signatures, to be valid, must be written in cursive script, not printed.

Because Palmer had made the decision to run for state senate at the last minute, her signatures had been gathered hastily. Not enough of them were valid, and so she was disqualified from running. In fact, all of the other Democratic candidates were disqualified, too, by irregularities in their petitions. Obama ran unopposed in the Democratic primary. Since the Thirteenth District was heavily Democratic, he won the general election in November by a wide margin.

However, Obama was not welcomed with open arms when he took office in Springfield, the capital of Illinois. Some black politicians close to Alice Palmer felt he should have stepped aside rather than running against her. They thought Obama was more interested in his own ambition than in the good of the black community. At one point, another state senator heckled Obama so badly that they had a shouting match on the floor of the senate.

Another reason for Illinois legislators to dislike Obama was that he was critical of Illinois state politics. They resented his attitude. The fact that Obama had a law degree from Harvard only made them think of him as elitist.

There was a great deal to criticize about Illinois politics, which had a reputation for corruption. Also, there was continual fighting between groups: between Democrats and Republicans, and among the representatives of different districts. Obama wondered, with all the problems facing the state as a whole, why couldn't the politicians work together to solve them? For instance, unemployment was a problem for whites as well as blacks.

Some in the black community mistrusted Obama's approach. For many years, black politicians had had to struggle against the white power structure to achieve anything for their people. Now Obama was saying that multicultural cooperation was the best way for both blacks and whites to make progress. That sounded like

94

he was going over to the other side. The fact that many of his backers were white liberals made some blacks even more suspicious.

However, Obama went quietly to work. In 1998, he helped to get a campaign finance reform law passed in the Illinois legislature. The law, which prohibited legislators from accepting gifts from state contractors or lobbyists, passed the state senate easily. But Obama made some enemies among politicians who had benefited from such gifts.

Gradually, Obama got a reputation in the Illinois senate, at least among Republicans and downstate Democrats, for fair and reasonable dealing. "The most important thing that you do in Springfield is you bring all sides of an issue to the table and you make them feel they are being listened to," he explained to a journalist. It was the same approach that had worked well for Obama back at Harvard Law School, when he was the president of the *Harvard Law Review.*

Obama also made an effort to socialize with his fellow legislators. He began to play golf, a popular sport among the politicians. He joined a running poker game, which helped him make some friends among Republicans as well as Democrats, even though he often won. He still played basketball for fun and exercise, sometimes with a fellow legislator.

In 1998, Barack and Michelle Obama's daughter Malia Ann was born on the Fourth of July. In the midst of his joy, Obama was determined to be the kind of father that he wished he'd had. Writing *Dreams from My Father*, he'd thought long and hard about his childhood.

Barack's father had left him and his mother. His step-father had withdrawn as Barack grew older. His grand-father hadn't been able to make a good living, and his grandmother had supported the three of them. Barack didn't doubt that his father, his stepfather, and his grand-father Dunham had all loved him, but he felt he could do better by his own children.

As Obama quickly realized, being a good father and husband was not easy to balance with being a dedicated politician. For one thing, the legislature was in Spring-field, two hundred miles from their home in Chicago. Barack often had to be away from home overnight, leav-ing Michelle to change diapers and get up when the baby cried in the middle of the night.

Michelle cut back her work to a part-time job at the University of Chicago, but even so, she was tired and stressed. Barack, besides his work as state senator, still taught constitutional law at the University of Chicago. When he was home, he had paperwork to do or evening meetings to go to.

In spite of concerns about his family life, Obama didn't give up his ambition to rise in the political world. During his first two-year term, he took some time to travel around the southern half of Illinois. The people there weren't his constituents, but some of the issues he voted on in the legislature affected them, too. Also, they might become his constituents in the future, if he ran for a statewide office.

In contrast to the big city of Chicago, central and southern Illinois were made up of farming communities and small cities. Although those areas were mainly Republican, middle-class, and white, Obama found that he felt comfortable with the downstate voters. In fact, they reminded him of his grandparents from the Midwest, Stanley and Madelyn Dunham.

CHAPTER 11

STATE SENATOR OBAMA

BARACK OBAMA NEVER INTENDED TO REMAIN IN the Illinois state senate forever. Originally, he'd thought he would follow in Harold Washington's footsteps to become a progressive mayor of Chicago. But by now Richard M. Daley was mayor, and he seemed to have a firm political hold on the city for the foreseeable future. It would be foolish, Barack judged, to try to challenge Daley.

However, Obama thought he saw a good opportunity to run for U.S. House of Representatives in 2000. Obama had the impression that the current congressman for the First District, Representative Bobby Rush, could be unseated. Obama didn't think Rush had accomplished much during his several years in Congress. Obama felt he couldn't pass up such a good political chance, even though he and Michelle were in the middle of adjusting to parenthood.

But before long Obama realized that Congressman Rush was more secure in his seat than he'd first assumed. For one thing, all the voters knew who Bobby Rush was, while hardly any of them had heard of Barack Obama. Not only that but the polls showed voters giving Rush a good solid 70 percent approval rating.

Rush was unquestionably part of the black community he represented. He'd worked in the civil rights movement of the 1960s. He was a former member of the Black Panthers, an organization formed to promote civil rights and self-defense for African-Americans. Also, Rush had been a close political ally of the late beloved black mayor of Chicago, Harold Washington.

Obama, in contrast, was easily portrayed by his opponents as "not black enough." It wasn't so much about his white mother as it was about his elite Columbia and Harvard education and the fact that he talked as if he were white. Furthermore, some of his biggest campaign contributors were well-to-do whites, like the real estate developers who were reaping profits from turning run-down South Side neighborhoods into upscale areas. Such development was resisted by black activists, since one effect was poor black renters being pushed out of these neighborhoods.

Another drawback for Obama was his lack of campaign funds. Running for U.S. representative took much more money than running for state senator. Especially since he wasn't well-known, Obama needed a good media blitz to get his name into voters' heads. In order to run enough television ads, he'd need at least $200,000 a week. But his fund for the entire campaign amounted to only $600,000.

Besides these disadvantages, Obama had two strokes of bad luck. First, Bobby Rush's son was shot and killed on the street. There was a flood of public sympathy for Rush, the grieving father. In other circumstances, the best tactic for an underdog like Obama to beat a frontrunner like Rush would have been to attack him vigorously. But now it would look very bad if Obama criticized his rival, so he held back.

Next, in December 1999, Obama, Michelle, and Malia (then almost a year and a half old) left for a vacation in Hawaii. Christmas in Hawaii with his grandmother, now in bad health, was a longstanding tradition for Barack. This year, he and Michelle needed the vacation more than usual, with the added strains of his campaign and of caring for a toddler. Barack originally planned to stay in Hawaii for two weeks, but he cut the trip to five days because of his campaign schedule.

Unfortunately, while Obama was away, an important vote came up in the Illinois senate: the Safe Neighborhoods gun-control bill. The murder rate in Chicago was higher than ever, and the issue was underlined by Bobby Rush's son's recent death by shooting. Voters in Obama's district supported the measure, and so did he—he'd always been in favor of gun control.

Obama's campaign manager, Dan Shomon, urged him to fly back to Illinois for the vote. That was what Obama wanted to do, since he knew the vote would be close. But Michelle was unhappy that he was spending so much time away from the family, and now Malia had come down with a bad cold. Obama stayed in Hawaii—and the Safe Neighborhoods measure failed to pass by three votes.

Returning the following week at the beginning of January 2000, Obama explained to the media about his commitment to his grandmother, his wife, and his sick child. But only one message got across to voters: State Senator Obama had stayed in Hawaii, probably lounging on the beach sipping tropical drinks, while a desperately needed anticrime bill went down in defeat in Springfield. Even the *Chicago Tribune*, which favored Obama's candidacy for Congress, scolded that he had chosen "a trip to Hawaii over public safety in Illinois."

At this point Obama knew that his campaign for U.S. congressman had failed. Almost worse, he knew he'd have to go on campaigning, smiling and shaking hands and giving upbeat speeches, as if he thought he were going to win. It was painfully hard. The night of the primary election a couple of months later, he wasn't surprised when he lost to Bobby Rush by thirty-one points.

After this humiliating defeat, Barack Obama spent the next few years working steadily in the state senate. He still had big ambitions about where he could go in politics and what he could accomplish, but he'd learned important lessons. One was about timing—it hadn't been the right time for him to run for Congress, after all. He had to be more patient.

Another lesson Obama learned was about how to campaign. He had a tendency to speak to political audiences the same way he spoke to his University of Chicago classes on constitutional law. Obama was a popular lecturer at the law school, but graduate-level speeches didn't go over as well with the general public. His speeches had to be less intellectual and more about his plans to change voters' lives for the better.

Also, as Jeremiah Wright advised Obama, he had to work harder on building a support network among the people in his party. Obama realized this was true. For instance, Emil Jones, the leader of the Democrats in the state senate, had a great deal of influence. Obama made an effort to get to know Jones and to work with him.

On June 10, 2001, Michelle and Barack's second daughter, Natasha (nicknamed "Sasha"), was born. Now Obama's family needed him more than ever. If he continued to climb the political ladder, he would have less and less time for his personal life. Still, Obama was seriously considering running for U.S. senator in 2004. The Republican senator from Illinois, Peter Fitzgerald, was up for reelection, and he didn't have much support from either his party or his constituents.

When Sasha was just three months old, she came down with meningitis, a sometimes-fatal inflammation of the membrane around the brain and spinal cord. Fortunately, Barack was home at the time. He and Michelle rushed the baby to the hospital and stayed there with her for three days. Barack Obama was a fiercely ambitious, focused, disciplined politician, but in Sasha's hospital room he didn't think about his political future at all.

Shortly after the Obamas' personal crisis, the attacks of September 11, 2001, shook the nation. Barack was in Chicago at the time, and he heard the first reports on his car radio that morning as he drove to a state legislature hearing. Then, with the rest of America, he watched the nightmarish scenes on TV of the hijacked planes crashing into the World Trade Center in New York. He watched the Twin Towers, a symbol of American economic power, crumble, and the Pentagon, the center of American military might, burst into flames. The sights struck fear into all American hearts.

Most state legislators didn't feel called upon to make a public response to the disaster. But Barack Obama was already thinking in wider terms than his state senate district in Illinois. He wrote a thoughtful piece about 9/11, as the event came to be called, for the *Hyde Park Herald*.

Obama noted that the United States needed to increase national security and make sure that al-Qaeda, the terrorist group that had mounted the suicide attacks on the United States, could not launch another attack. But Americans also needed to examine "the sources of such madness," he said. They needed to "devote far more attention to the monumental task of raising the hopes and prospects of embittered children across the globe—children not just in the Middle East, but also in Africa, Asia, Latin America, Eastern Europe and within our own shores."

The aftermath of 9/11 affected not only the United States but also the rest of the world. The stock market plunged. President George W. Bush launched a "War on Terror," beginning with a mission to Afghanistan to hunt down the terrorists. Congress quickly passed a measure to add a new department, Homeland Security, to the federal government.

Among all the far-reaching damage caused by the attacks of 9/11, there was one small coincidence that affected Barack Obama in particular. As a media consultant told him soon after September 11, 2001, the "political dynamics" had changed. Barack Obama the politician had just been hit by some personal bad luck.

What the consultant meant was that the chief of al-Qaeda happened to be named Osama bin Laden. No matter that Barack Obama, American-born, had gotten his name from his Kenyan father, while Osama bin Laden was Saudi Arabian. To most Americans, "Osama" and "Obama" were both strange, foreign names that sounded almost the same. And "Osama" was a name that called up hate and fear.

Michelle and everyone else, including Shomon, Obama's chief of staff, advised him against entering the Senate race in 2004. But Obama argued that this was his best chance for a political career. If he didn't make his move now, he might as well give up politics and practice law instead.

There was one possible hitch: Democrat Carol Moseley Braun might decide to run. Braun had served as senator from Illinois from 1993 to 1999, the first African-American woman to reach the Senate. Now she was thinking of trying to take back her Senate seat. Braun, not only former senator but also former U.S. ambassador to New Zealand, would have been hard for any other Democrat to beat in the primary election. Obama knew she'd have full support from both the black voters and the wealthy white liberals in Chicago.

As Obama waited for Carol Moseley Braun to make up her mind, he promised Michelle that if he ran and lost, he'd forget about politics. He'd concentrate on a career that fit better with their home life and made more money. Money was a big factor, since Barack Obama's ill-fated campaign for congressman in 2000, although it was underfunded, had cost almost $550,000. Some of that money had come from his own pocket, and the Obamas were still paying off those debts.

Barack suggested to Michelle that if he won the Senate seat, he could write a book and make a lot of money. Michelle, the practical one in their marriage, seriously doubted that—of course he *could* write a book, but most books didn't make money. Look at *Dreams from My Father*. However, by the end of the summer of 2002, Michelle agreed to this one last political campaign.

Part of Obama's motivation for wanting to take part in national politics, and the motivation of people supporting him, was dismay at the political decisions that were now being made in Washington. Throughout the summer and fall of 2002, the Bush administration argued that Saddam Hussein's Iraq possessed weapons of mass destruction, including perhaps nuclear weapons. They also suggested that Iraq had direct links with al-Qaeda, the terrorists who had plotted the 9/11 attacks. President Bush urged Congress to authorize him to use force against Iraq. On October 10 and 11, Congress voted by a wide majority to give the president the power to use force if necessary to disarm Iraq.

Barack Obama thought this measure was a serious

107

mistake, and so did the growing group of antiwar activists in Chicago. They asked him to speak at an antiwar rally in Chicago later in October 2002. Obama worked hard on his speech, carefully spelling out why he opposed invading Iraq. It wasn't because he was against *all* wars, he said. "What I am opposed to is a dumb war."

Obama was skeptical about the Bush administration's evidence that Saddam Hussein possessed weapons of mass destruction. He also thought they were being unrealistic about how easily the war could be won or how much it would cost. He believed they were pursuing the war for political reasons. And he believed the war would increase the instability of the Middle East—and even increase terrorism.

In December 2002, Barack took his family to Hawaii for Christmas as usual. He was still there when he got the news that Carol Moseley Braun had decided to run for president—not senator—in 2004. This was the moment Obama was waiting for.

CHAPTER 12

BIG-TIME POLITICS

IN JANUARY 2003, BARACK OBAMA ANNOUNCED HIS candidacy for the U.S. Senate. Several other candidates for the Democratic nomination also declared, but none of them was as formidable an opponent as Carol Moseley Braun would have been.

Obama hired a high-powered staff for his campaign, beginning with media consultant David Axelrod. Axelrod was an experienced and sought-after political consultant, especially gifted at creating TV ads for his clients. He had worked on the U.S. Senate campaigns of Paul Simon of Illinois, Christopher Dodd of Connecticut, and Hillary Clinton of New York, as well as on many others'.

Axelrod could pick and choose the candidates he wanted to work for, so it was telling that he chose new-comer Barack Obama. Obama couldn't afford to pay him as much as some other candidates could, but Axelrod was impressed with Obama's political talent, and he sincerely believed that it was important for Obama to be elected. "I thought that if I could help Barack Obama get to Washington, then I would have accomplished something great in my life," he later told an interviewer. With Axelrod on board, Obama could attract many other top professionals, such as communications director Robert Gibbs, to his campaign.

Obama had important supporters among other politicians, including Emil Jones, the leader of the Democrats in the Illinois state senate. The Reverend Jesse Jackson Sr. would also use his influence to support Obama. Jackson, the best-known black leader in America, had worked for civil rights ever since the 1960s, and he had twice run for president in the Democratic primaries. His daughter Santita Jackson, a childhood friend of Michelle's, had sung at Michelle and Barack's wedding.

Paul Simon, now a popular former senator, also intended to support Obama. Unfortunately, Simon died suddenly in December 2003, but the fact of his approval helped Obama's candidacy anyway.

At the beginning of his campaign for the U.S. Senate,

BARACK**OBAMA**

Obama had to face a hard fact: he was going to need a lot
of money. As he explained to a gathering of his financial
backers, just to have a good chance of winning the election, he'd need $5 million. But if he could raise $10 million, he guaranteed that he would win.

Not being well-known, Barack Obama didn't have
many wealthy donors eager to contribute to his campaign.
He had to make phone call after phone call to people
who might perhaps be persuaded to contribute, knowing
that most of them wouldn't even bother to return his call.
The humiliating experience reminded him of when he
was living with his grandparents in Hawaii and listening
to his grandfather Stanley calling up people to sell them
life insurance.

Happily, as the campaign went on, word of mouth
began to spread that Obama was an unusually talented and
exciting candidate. More people with money came forward to contribute. Also, through appeals on the Internet,
Obama gathered numerous smaller donations, and that
signaled widespread support for his candidacy. At this time,
the idea of raising political funds through the Internet was
fairly new.

From the beginning of his campaign, Barack Obama

9

spent nearly every Sunday morning giving talks in black churches around Chicago. He told these audiences that he was a member of Trinity United Church of Christ and that his pastor was the popular preacher Jeremiah Wright. He also filled the congregations in on his background in civil rights: his involvement with the antiapartheid movement, his work as a community organizer in Chicago, and his increasingly impressive record as a state senator.

In 2003 the Democrats gained the majority in the Illinois state senate. That meant that Emil Jones became president of the senate, with the power to assign responsibility for a bill. Working with Jones, Obama sponsored almost eight hundred bills in two years.

More than 280 of these bills became law, and several of them were important gains for civil rights. One law discouraged police from using racial profiling to pull drivers over. Another required the police to videotape prisoners' confessions. Another law expanded the state's health insurance to cover thousands more poor children.

Health insurance was a major issue with Barack Obama, not just for residents of Illinois but also for everyone in the country. It was one of the reasons he was eager to enter the senate, to have a hand in reforming the U.S. health-care system. In November 2003 he was appalled when Congress passed the Medicare Prescription Drug, Improvement, and Modernization Act. He wrote later that this law, supposedly an improvement in the health-care system, "somehow managed to combine the worst aspects of the public and private sectors—price gouging and bureaucratic confusion, gaps in coverage and an eye-popping bill for taxpayers."

Obama also had a strong interest in foreign policy, even aside from the Iraq War. He was very concerned about Sudan, a country in northeastern Africa where a bloody civil war burst out at the beginning of 2003. The Sudanese government, together with the militia, killed hundreds of thousands of people in the Darfur region and made refugees out of millions more. Obama felt that the United States should give more attention to such a massive humanitarian crisis.

As Obama gave speech after speech on the campaign trail, Axelrod counseled him to make his speeches more personal. Obama had a rich baritone voice, like his father, and he was an articulate speaker, but he still had a tendency to get too intellectual. With reminders from Michelle and from his staff, he worked on connecting with his audiences' daily lives.

Since a senatorial race requires many television appearances in advertisements, interviews, and debates, it was a big advantage that Obama came across well on TV. He had a gift for communicating his sincerity and idealism. He gave an impression of serenity—a deep calm and inner strength—even under the stress of campaigning. When Obama's political consultants conducted a focus-group test, one woman remarked that Obama reminded her of the African-American movie star Sidney Poitier.

In his basic campaign speech, Obama started by joking about his name. Everyone knew his name was a disadvantage for a politician, so he brought up the subject himself. People were always getting his last name wrong, he said, garbling it as "Yo mama" or "Alabama." Or they thought it was Irish—O'Bama?

Then he explained that Obama was his Kenyan family name, that "Barack" meant "blessed"—and by the way, his mother was from Kansas. This speech opener gave his audience a quick biography sketch, and it also gained sympathy for him because he was laughing at himself.

David Axelrod produced a series of TV advertisements for Obama, using the theme "Yes, we can." The ads emphasized Obama's Harvard education, which tended to appeal to white voters; his work as a community organizer in Chicago, which tended to appeal to black voters; and his idealism, which appealed to both groups. In the closing, Obama spoke directly to the camera, with quiet conviction. "Now they say we can't change Washington? I'm Barack Obama. I'm running for the United States Senate, and I approve this message to say, 'Yes, we can.'"

When Axelrod first proposed the "Yes, we can" theme, Obama didn't like it. He thought it was too simple. But Michelle thought it was a good slogan for him, so he trusted her judgment. In fact, "Yes, we can" had wide appeal, and the TV ads were very effective.

Meanwhile, Obama's two main Democratic opponents, Dan Hynes and Blair Hull, had spent most of their time attacking each other. As the date of the primary election approached, the polls showed Obama in the lead. Not only that, but it was becoming evident that he had star power. As the *Chicago Sun-Times* put it in a story about personable Chicago politicians, "The first African-American president of the *Harvard Law Review* has a movie-star smile and more than a little mystique."

On primary election day in March, Barack Obama voted and then played basketball to relax and take his mind off the campaign. That night, as the results came in, Obama's supporters went wild with delight. He was sweeping the black precincts, but he was also sweeping the precincts that were mainly white. In spite of Chicago's bitter history of racial politics, Obama seemed to be a candidate with universal appeal. And that fact gave people hope for overcoming the bitterness, making Obama all the more attractive.

At Barack Obama's victory party, Michelle, Malia, Sasha, Maya, and Michelle's brother, Craig, joined him onstage. Barack spoke to the overjoyed crowd, and they responded with a chant: "Yes, we can! Yes, we can!"

As the general election campaign began, Obama's Republican rival, Jack Ryan, seemed like a strong opponent. Like Obama, he was young and good-looking, but he also had the personal wealth to spend on a political race. One way Ryan used his money was to hire a cameraman to follow Obama around everywhere he went. The idea was partly to watch for any embarrassing slip Obama might make, and partly to get on his nerves.

The cameraman, sometimes from as close as five feet, filmed Obama's private phone conversations with his wife. He followed him into elevators to film him. He even filmed Obama coming out of the restroom.

Finally Obama turned the tables on Ryan. Leading his cameraman stalker into the press office of the state capitol, he introduced him to a roomful of reporters. The reporters jumped on the story, TV camera crews appeared, and the news story of the day became Ryan unfairly harassing Obama.

But a much more damaging revelation about Jack Ryan was that recently he had gone through a messy divorce from his wife, a Hollywood actress. The media leaped on that story, too, keeping it in the news not only in Illinois but nationwide. By June, Jack Ryan had lost all support, even among Republicans, and he was forced to drop out of the race.

It now seemed certain that Barack Obama would win the general election in November, but the Obama campaign didn't slow down. His staff worked to get him a chance to speak at the Democratic National Convention in Boston at the end of July. As it so happened, the Democratic candidate for president, John Kerry, had met Obama and was impressed with him. Also, the Democratic National Committee wanted to showcase a minority, someone well-spoken, at the convention. In the end, they offered him the keynote speech of the convention.

This was a great opportunity for a state senator, or even a new U.S. senator. Obama's audience for the keynote speech would be not only the five thousand delegates to the convention but also television viewers across the United States. Depending on how well he spoke, Barack could become a national political star—or a big flop.

Now Obama was in the limelight all the time, and he felt the strain. He was tired but at the same time driven on by nervous energy. His week at the Democratic National Convention began with an appearance on NBC's *Meet the Press*, where he calmly and skillfully answered questions from Tim Russert, a famously tough interviewer. Everywhere he went in the convention center, his staff had to fend off media journalists, photographers, and autograph seekers. In private moments, he worked on his speech.

Obama was a talented writer and speaker in his own right, and he didn't do well if he had to speak someone else's words. So he wrote the speech himself, using input and feedback from his staff and Michelle, as well as some editing from John Kerry's staff.

Tuesday night, just before he was scheduled to go onstage, Barack Obama sat with Michelle for a rare private moment. He wore a dark suit that he'd chosen himself, and the light blue striped tie that his communications director, Gibbs, had been wearing. David Axelrod had thought Obama's own patterned tie was too nondescript and insisted that he change ties with Gibbs. Michelle, who had a strong fashion sense, agreed. It was a small detail, but in this big moment every little detail counted.

Barack had remained amazingly calm up to this point, but now he was nervous. Michelle gave him a hug and teased, "Just don't screw it up, buddy!" It was the right thing to say to break the tension, and they both laughed.

In fact, Barack Obama's speech was an enormous success. The crowd that filled Boston's FleetCenter arena was longing for an uplifting, inspiring speech, and Obama gave it to them. He talked about his family: his Kenyan grandfather, who had big dreams for his goat-herding son; his grandparents from Kansas, who had expected a bright career for their daughter; and his Kenyan father and American mother, who could trust that their mixed-race son, from a family of modest means, would be educated in the best schools in that generous country, America. "This is the true genius of America," he told the audience, "a faith in the simple dreams of the people."

To a country weary of partisan politics, he spoke

of "a belief that we are connected as one people." He asserted, "There's not a liberal America and a conservative America—there's the United States of America. There's not a black America and white America and Latino America and Asian America—there's the United States of America." He spoke of unity, and the "politics of hope" to replace the "politics of cynicism."

The audience responded by jumping to their feet, shouting, and bursting into tears. Veteran TV newsmen like MSNBC's Chris Matthews and CNN's Wolf Blitzer were deeply impressed. As for Michelle, she ran onstage with tears on her face, too, and hugged him again.

Madelyn Dunham, watching her grandson on TV in Hawaii, called him up to say, "You did well." Obama knew that, coming from Toot, that was big praise—she wasn't one to jump up and down or burst into tears. In case she'd praised him too much, she added, "I just kind of worry about you. I hope you keep your head on straight." But later she admitted to a reporter that she thought it was "really quite an exceptional speech."

In spite of Obama's triumph at the Democratic convention, he still had to win the senatorial race in Illinois. The Republicans came up with a new opponent for Obama:

Alan Keyes. Keyes was an African–American conservative from Maryland. Even the Republican party did not expect Keyes to win the election, and polls soon showed Obama way ahead.

However, Keyes was a fiery speaker, and the Republicans hoped he might burn off a bit of Obama's glow. But although he attacked Obama vigorously, voters didn't pay much attention. In November, Barack Obama won by a landslide.

John Kerry, in contrast, lost the presidential election. President George W. Bush's popularity had dwindled during his first term, but Americans were still worried about the threat of terrorism after the 9/11 attacks. They saw President Bush as more likely to keep America safe than Senator Kerry, who criticized the ongoing Iraq War.

Also, although many Americans were dissatisfied with George W. Bush as the nation's leader, they didn't see Kerry as a better replacement. Kerry, who had been in the Senate since 1984, seemed like an all-too-familiar Washington politician. He didn't have charisma, or the gift of connecting with audiences and inspiring them. John Kerry didn't offer Americans the image of the leader they were looking for.

CHAPTER 13

SENATOR OBAMA

ON JANUARY 4, 2005, A MILD, SUNNY DAY IN Washington, D.C., Barack Obama was sworn in as a new member of the United States Senate. He was the only African-American member of the Senate at this time, and he was only the third African-American to be elected to the office since Reconstruction ended in 1877. Michelle, Malia, and Sasha cheered him on from the gallery, and so did Maya, Auma, and Auma's mother, Kezia.

Then Michelle and the girls went back to Chicago, and Barack tried to get used to living on his own in Washington for most of each week. He'd wanted to move the family to Washington, because he knew how much he would miss them, but finally he'd agreed with Michelle that it was better to keep their residence in Chicago, where they had a solid network of family and friends.

The most important person in the Chicago network was Marian Robinson. Michelle's mother loved spending time with Malia and Sasha, and the girls were comfortable and happy with her. Since Marian lived only ten minutes away from the Obamas, she could easily drive the girls to lessons, sports, or friends' houses. Or she could stay overnight with them if Michelle had to be away from home.

Now that the family was in the public eye so much, Michelle felt that they needed a larger home for privacy. In June that year the Obamas bought a stately three-story house, almost a hundred years old, in Hyde Park, not far from the University of Chicago. They could afford to buy a big house because Barack's huge success at the Democratic National Convention had given new life to his book. The paperback publisher of *Dreams from My Father* reissued the book, and it began to sell wildly. The publisher then offered Obama a contract for three more books, with an advance of almost $2 million. Barack's unlikely scheme to solve their financial problems by writing a book had turned out much better than Michelle expected.

Barack rented an apartment in Washington, and he stayed there during the week, when Congress was in session. Weekends he spent in Chicago. He always had official obligations on Saturday, but he saved Sundays for Michelle and their daughters.

At the same time that he was beginning this high-pressure new job, Obama was also writing his next book. The book contract with its large advance had solved the Obamas' money problems, but it only added to the problem of the many demands on his time. Obama titled the new book *The Audacity of Hope*, using a memorable phrase from one of Jeremiah Wright's sermons at Trinity Church.

During his first years in the Senate, Barack Obama worked quietly and tried to keep a low profile. Most of the time, he voted with the rest of the Democrats. An exception was the Military Commissions Act of 2006, which allowed the military to imprison indefinitely, without a hearing, anyone the federal government termed an "unlawful enemy combatant." Obama was one of only thirty-four senators to oppose the act, believing that it violated civil liberties guaranteed by the United States Constitution and encouraged the harsh interrogation of prisoners.

True to his promise to work for unity, against partisan politics, Obama teamed with Republicans on a number of bills. His main accomplishment was a bill he cosponsored with Republican senator Richard Lugar of Indiana, the respected chairman of the Senate Foreign Relations Committee. Lugar knew that Obama admired the work that he and Senator Sam Nunn had already done on controlling the world's stockpiles of nuclear weapons. He encouraged Obama to join the Foreign Relations Committee and invited him to cosponsor the Lugar-Obama Nonproliferation Initiative, a follow-up to the Nunn-Lugar Cooperative Threat Reduction program.

To gather information for their bill, Obama traveled with Lugar to Russia in 2005. They viewed warehouses full of nuclear missiles, now being closely guarded and dismantled under the Nunn-Lugar program. In neighboring Ukraine, formerly part of the Soviet Union, they saw poorly guarded stores of land mines, as well as of the biological weapon anthrax, and realized how easily terrorists could seize them. The Lugar-Obama Nonproliferation Initiative aimed to reduce worldwide stockpiles of both conventional weapons and weapons of mass destruction. The bill would finally become law in January 2007.

Obama was still traveling with Senator Lugar in Europe on August 29, 2005, when one of the worst natural disasters in U.S. history hit the Gulf Coast. Hurricane Katrina made landfall in Mississippi and Louisiana, the levees protecting New Orleans failed, and the city was flooded. Almost two thousand people died in the disaster, and tens of thousands lost their homes. The hurricane caused more than $80 billion in damage, making it the costliest natural disaster in U.S. history.

Although the National Hurricane Center and the National Weather Service had given plenty of warning, the city, state, and federal governments were all slow to respond. TV news programs showed shocking scenes of helpless elderly people waiting in wheelchairs in the smothering heat, of bodies floating past flooded neighborhoods, of looters raiding abandoned stores. About twenty thousand refugees huddled in the Louisiana Superdome, the main sports center in New Orleans, without enough food, water, or sanitation.

The Federal Emergency Management Agency (FEMA) was bitterly criticized, and the Bush administration was accused of racism, since the people who suffered most from the effects of the hurricane were poor and black. The hip-hop artist Kanye West said bluntly, "George Bush doesn't care about black people."

Interviewed on ABC's TV program *This Week with*

George Stephanopoulos, Obama responded thoughtfully. When he'd returned from Europe, he had visited the Astrodome in Houston, Texas, where thousands of the refugees were sheltered. He saw that the refugees were like many of the inner-city people he had worked with in Chicago—poor, badly educated, in ill health. They had been barely hanging on, even before the hurricane struck. "We didn't have nothin' before the storm," one woman told him. "Now we got less than nothin'."

It wasn't so much that the federal government was racist, Obama explained to George Stephanopoulos. Instead, it was composed of people who were incompetent and completely out of touch with the way poor people in a city like New Orleans actually lived. He thought that "whoever was in charge of planning was so detached from the realities of inner-city life in a place like New Orleans that they couldn't conceive of the notion that somebody couldn't load up their SUV, put one hundred dollars' worth of gas in there, put [in] some sparkling water, and drive off to a hotel and check in with a credit card."

In August 2006 Senator Obama took an official trip to Africa as a congressional delegation. He had planned this trip since the beginning of 2005. It would be a fact-finding mission about the AIDS epidemic in many African countries and the gross human rights violations in Darfur.

The first country on Obama's route was South Africa. Near Cape Town, he toured the prison where Nelson Mandela, hero of the antiapartheid resistance, had been held for eighteen of his twenty-seven years of imprisonment. This was a moving moment for Obama, who had first been drawn into politics over the issue of apartheid in South Africa.

The next day he visited a health center in a shantytown area outside Cape Town. There he spoke to reporters about the acute epidemic of AIDS, one of the worst in the world, from which South Africans were suffering. The president of South Africa, Thabo Mbeki, had doubted in a public statement that the disease of AIDS was caused by the HIV infection, although this was an established medical fact.

Obama hoped to meet with Mbeki during his visit, and he didn't want to offend him. But he felt that AIDS was too grave a threat to be polite about. He criticized Mbeki's government sharply as being "in denial" of scientific facts about AIDS, and he called for a "sense of urgency." The next day, Mbeki refused to meet with Obama. However, many other South Africans were grateful to him for speaking out.

After four days in South Africa, Obama flew to Kenya. Michelle, Malia, and Sasha joined him for this part of the trip. So did his half sister Auma, who was now living near London and working in social services. Barack was eager to show his children the country of their grandfather Obama and introduce them to their Kenyan relatives. Obama also hoped, as he explained at a news conference in Nairobi, to be "a bridge between the two nations" with this official trip to Kenya.

As it soon became apparent, the media attention during the visit was so intense that the Obamas had almost no personal time. Also, everywhere Barack Obama went in Kenya, he was greeted by adoring crowds. To Kenyans, he was an American prince. In Nairobi a young man in the crowd held aloft an oil portrait of Obama that he had painted. Obama in the picture had a glow around him, almost as if he were a saint.

Obama and his family made the trip from Nairobi to his father's childhood home in Kolego, as Obama had done in 1988 and 1991. The difference was that the first two trips had been private, but this one was overwhelmingly public. Instead of traveling with Auma by bus with chickens on his lap, as he had in 1988, Obama flew from Nairobi followed by a huge press corps.

As the centerpiece of their visit to Obama's ancestral home, Barack and Michelle planned to have their blood tested for AIDS at a provincial medical clinic. They wanted to make the point that anyone could—and should—get tested for AIDS. Thousands of Kenyans crowded the streets on the way to the clinic, dancing and chanting, "Everything is possible with Obama." Camera crews and reporters struggled through the cheering throngs to watch the test in a trailer provided by the U.S. Centers for Disease Control and Prevention (CDC). The CDC estimated that half a million more people might have gotten themselves tested, just as a result of the Obamas' demonstration.

Next, Obama and his family visited a CARE Kenya project far out in the bush. This project was also connected with the AIDS crisis, enabling older women to support children orphaned by AIDS. Obama himself had provided part of the funding for the project, which gave money to the women to invest in equipment such as sewing machines.

At the gathering of the women and children involved

in the CARE project, Obama was honored with worship-
ful dancing and singing. Michelle said to a reporter, "It's all
a bit overwhelming." The intense attention and adulation
continued to be overwhelming as the Obamas proceeded
to a school in Kogelo, the village near his family compound. Obama had donated money to the school, and it
was named after him: the Senator Obama Kogelo Second-
ary School. Thousands of Luo tribespeople had gathered
here for a combined celebration of Obama's visit and a
political rally for the upcoming Kenyan elections.

After ceremonies at the school, the Obamas then drove
the short distance to the Obama family compound, where
Barack's Kenyan grandmother, Granny, greeted them. She
was now eighty-three. Barack had planned that he and
Michelle and their daughters would spend more than two
hours in private with her. But because of the crowds and
the reporters and cameras waiting, they had only forty
minutes, barely enough time to eat a meal together.

At the end of their Kenya visit, the Obamas took two
days to enjoy a safari in Masai country. Then Barack and
Michelle flew northwest to Chad, where they visited a
refugee camp filled with victims of the civil war in neighboring Sudan. Obama had planned to visit Darfur itself,

but the Sudanese government refused to let him into the country. More than 200,000 refugees from Darfur lived in camps like this in the desert, surviving on rations and water trucked in by the UN.

By visiting the camp and talking with some of the refugees, Obama hoped to learn more about Darfur. But the visit was frustrating, because he had less than two hours to listen to the refugees, and their stories had to be translated from Arabic to French to English for him. However, he hoped that his appearance would draw more media attention to the plight of the refugees.

In October 2006, soon after Barack Obama returned from Africa, his new book was published. *The Audacity of Hope: Thoughts on Reclaiming the American Dream* was an immediate success. It wasn't as personal a book as *Dreams from My Father*, but it was still much more straightforward and readable than the usual politician's book. It expressed, in more detail, the themes of his speech at the Democratic National Convention in 2004: We are one nation. Our best comes out in working together for the common good. Everyone deserves a fair chance at the American dream.

In *The Audacity of Hope*, Obama sharply criticized

many of the policies of the Bush administration, especially the Iraq War. Obama had opposed the war as long ago as the fall of 2002, before the war was even officially launched. Now he pointed out that the Iraq War was only one example of the Bush administration's confused foreign policy. For example, why invade Iraq but not North Korea? Kim Jong Il's government was just as repressive as Saddam Hussein's, and North Korea actually possessed weapons of mass destruction.

At the same time, Obama was careful to make the point that he didn't consider George W. Bush to be a bad man. In fact, he assumed that President Bush and the people in his administration were sincerely trying to do what they thought best for the country. In one-to-one meetings with Bush, Obama found the president friendly and likeable.

The Audacity of Hope also communicated Barack Obama's ability to laugh at himself. For example, he told about calling Michelle from Washington to bring her up-to-date about how his bill with Dick Lugar was going. Caught up in the work of the Senate, Barack couldn't imagine anything more important than the Nonproliferation Initiative.

But Michelle was on a different track, on which the most important issue was an ant invasion of their house.

She interrupted him with a request: Would he pick up some ant traps on his way home from Washington the next day? Bemused, Barack wondered whether famous senators like Edward Kennedy or John McCain ever had to buy ant traps after negotiating legislation of worldwide significance in the Senate. He could count on Michelle to bring him down to earth.

Obama wasn't up for reelection in 2006, since U.S. senators have six-year terms. But he helped other Democratic candidates campaign. To his satisfaction, the national elections in November gave the Democrats a majority in both the Senate and the House of Representatives. That, together with President Bush's continuing unpopularity, boded well for the Democrats to capture the White House in 2008.

CHAPTER 14

RUNNING FOR PRESIDENT

DURING THE FALL OF 2006, BARACK OBAMA TURNED
to the question of whether he should try to run for president in 2008. Although the election was more than two
years away, he needed to decide now. A presidential campaign would require an enormous effort, far beyond what
he and his supporters had done for his Senate race.

Obama consulted first with Michelle and with his
most trusted staff, David Axelrod and Robert Gibbs. Then
he went on to talk with a range of friends whose opinions
he respected, including the Reverends Jeremiah Wright
and Jesse Jackson. The feedback he got was very positive.

Although Barack Obama was young for the presidency—
he was forty-seven when inaugurated in 2009—he wasn't
as young as Theodore Roosevelt, the youngest president at
forty-two upon inauguration. John F. Kennedy had become

president at forty-three. Obama lacked experience at the national level of government, but JFK had served only two terms in the Senate. Abraham Lincoln had served only *one* term as congressman from Illinois before his election to the presidency.

One encouraging sign for Obama's candidacy was that his new book, *The Audacity of Hope*, was a runaway bestseller. This success gave him a great deal of good publicity. His face was on the cover of *Time* magazine, and his book tour included an appearance with Michelle on *Oprah*.

President George W. Bush's unpopularity was an advantage for any Democratic candidate. Bush himself wouldn't be able to run, since 2008 would be the end of his second four-year term. But the Republican candidate would have to struggle to avoid being linked with the problems of the Bush administration: the seemingly endless war in Iraq, the soaring national budget deficit, the sluggish economy.

In considering whether Barack should run for president, Michelle worried about the effects of his political career on their family. A presidential bid meant that Michelle, as well as Barack, had to spend the next two years campaigning. It meant even less privacy and time with each other and with their two young children.

Still, by December 2006, Michelle had agreed to support Barack in his bid for the presidency. She made him promise to stop smoking, however, before she promised to help him campaign. Also, she was determined to keep her children's lives stable, in spite of the tremendous pressures of their father's run for president.

To free up time for campaigning, Michelle quit her position on the board of TreeHouse, a supplier to Walmart Stores. She also cut back on her work as vice president at the University of Chicago Hospitals. And Marian Robinson, Michelle's mother, quit her job as a bank secretary. Now she could be available full-time for Malia and Sasha when Michelle and Barack were on the road.

As Obama prepared to begin his campaign for president, he received some bad publicity. Antoin "Tony" Rezko, a friend, fund-raiser, and heavy contributor to Obama's campaign for the Senate, was indicted for fraud in October 2006. (In June 2008 Rezko was convicted on sixteen counts of corruption.) In November 2006 it came out that in June 2005, at the same time that the Obamas bought their house in South Chicago, the Rezkos had bought the lot next door. Obama then bought a piece of Rezko's property to add to his yard, so that his children would have more room to play.

Obama hadn't done anything illegal or violated the Senate's ethics rules, but he admitted that he'd created the *appearance* that Rezko was doing him a favor by selling him part of his lot. This was a mistake, Obama said—"boneheaded," in fact. But if there had to be an embarrassing revelation, it was better to get it out of the way early in the campaign.

In February 2007 Barack Obama announced his candidacy for president of the United States. He made his announcement outside the Old State Capitol in Springfield, Illinois. "It's a little chilly today," he joked. (It was 12 degrees F.) "But I'm fired up." The cheering, beaming crowd of 15,000 was clearly fired up, too. As Obama reminded the audience, this site was where Abraham Lincoln had made his famous speech using the well-known quotation from the Bible: "A house divided against itself cannot stand."

Barack Obama was a bright new political star, and many commentators compared him with John F. Kennedy, also a handsome, inspiring young senator when he ran for president. But throughout 2007 the front-runner for the Democratic nomination was Senator Hillary Clinton of New York. As former First Lady for eight years during Bill Clinton's administration, she was much better known than Obama. Also, she had a powerful political organization in

Barack Obama at age nine with his mother, Ann Dunham; his sister, Maya; and his stepfather, Lolo, in 1970.

Barack Obama as a toddler with his mother.   Barack Obama Sr.

A rally for affirmative action and divestiture at Coons Hall at Occidental College in Los Angeles, California, in 1981. Barack Obama, seated on the right closest to the stage, will make his first public speech.

Barack Obama with his grandparents in New York City.

Barack Obama on the Harvard campus in Cambridge, Massachusetts, after he is named the president of the *Harvard Law Review* in 1990.

A young Barack and Michelle Obama spend Christmas in Hawaii.

Barack Obama speaks at the 2004 Democratic National Convention in Boston, Massachusetts, on July 27, 2004. His inspiring speech is an important landmark in his career.

Barack Obama is elected U.S. senator for Illinois on November 2, 2004. He celebrates with his wife, Michelle, and his daughters, Malia and Sasha, in Chicago.

As a U.S. senator, Barack Obama visits his step-grandmother, Sarah Obama, in Kenya on August 26, 2006.

Barack Obama makes history on November 4, 2008, when he wins the U.S. presidential election.

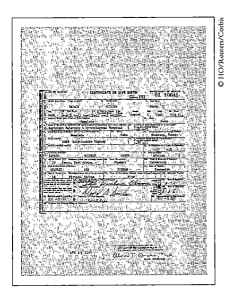

Barack Obama's birth certificate, released by the White House in response to Republican accusations that he was not born in the United States.

Barack Obama accepts the Nobel Peace Prize on December 10, 2009. He poses with the medal and the diploma in Oslo, Norway.

The nine Supreme Court Justices on September 29, 2009. First row, from left to right: Justice Anthony M. Kennedy, Justice John Paul Stevens, Chief Justice John Roberts, Justice Antonin Scalia, and Justice Clarence Thomas. Second row, from left to right: Justice Samuel Alito, Justice Ruth Bader Ginsburg, Justice Stephen G. Breyer, and Justice Sonia Sotomayor.

Barack Obama visits U.S. troops in Afghanistan on March 28, 2010.

Barack Obama wins a second term as U.S. president on November 7, 2012. He welcomes Vice President Joe Biden to the stage. Michelle, Sasha, and Malia Obama celebrate beside them.

The Occupy Wall Street encampment in Zuccotti Park in downtown New York City on November 4, 2011. Encampments like this were created all over the world as part of the global protest.

Members of the national security team are updated on the mission against Osama bin Laden in the White House's Situation Room on October 18, 2011. Vice President Joe Biden is on the far left, with President Obama to his left. Secretary of State Hillary Clinton sits across from them, with Secretary of Defense Robert Gates to her left.

Barack Obama leads a march across the Edmund Pettus Bridge in Selma, Alabama, to commemorate the fiftieth anniversary of the "Bloody Sunday" march from Selma to Montgomery in 1965.

place and the resources of her husband's backers.

However, Barack Obama's campaign quickly set a record for fund-raising, bringing in $58 million in the first half of 2007. An impressive number of the donations were from small donors, giving less than $200 each. Much of this money was raised through the Internet, since Obama's young campaign staffers were familiar with the Internet and knew how to use it. Through the Internet they were also able to quickly recruit and organize an army of volunteers.

Spontaneous Obama-supporting groups sprang up on social networking sites such as Facebook. By March 2007 there were more than five hundred Obama groups on Facebook. One of them, Students for Barack Obama, grew into a political action committee with almost 62,000 members.

Barack Obama's fame was also spread through an independently produced Internet video, "I Got a Crush . . . on Obama," first appearing on YouTube in June 2007. It was a comedic video making fun of how Obama's supporters swooned over him. It featured a young woman posing and singing provocatively against a background of Obama photos. This video was quickly viewed by millions of Americans and shown in TV news broadcasts. However, Obama wasn't pleased about the free publicity, because the video had upset Malia and Sasha. "You do wish people would think about what impact their actions have on kids and families," he said.

Michelle Obama campaigned vigorously for her husband, both in joint appearances and by herself. But the Obamas tried to keep their children's lives as normal as possible. Most of the time, Malia and Sasha stayed home in Chicago. "Our kids thrive on stability and routine and consistency," Michelle explained in an interview. Even during the summer of 2007, when the girls were out of school, Michelle planned their campaign trips around birthday parties and day-camp field trips.

Barack's American sister, Maya Soetoro-Ng, also campaigned for him, taking two months off from work. Even his grandmother Madelyn Dunham, although she was eighty-six and frail, took part in a TV advertisement for Obama.

As the primary election season opened in January 2008, Barack Obama began to draw even with Hillary Clinton. First he won the Iowa caucus. In the New Hampshire primary, although Clinton won the most votes, they won the same number of delegates to the Democratic National Convention. Obama congratulated Hillary Clinton on election night after the votes were in, but his speech to

140

his supporters sounded more like a victory speech than a concession. He used again the slogan that had been so successful in his campaign for the U.S. Senate: "Yes, we can." His audience roared back, "Yes—we—can!"

Obama went on to win the primaries in Nevada and South Carolina. On February 5, called Super Tuesday because so many states held their primary elections that day, Obama won twenty more delegates than Clinton. (By this time the Democratic candidate in third place, John Edwards, had dropped out of the race.) In a televised speech that night, even before all the returns were in, Obama talked about what he would do as president:

> I'll be a president who finally brings Democrats and Republicans together to make health care affordable and available for every single American. We will put a college education within reach of anyone who wants to go, and instead of just talking about how great our teachers are, we will reward them for their greatness, with more pay and better support. And we will harness the ingenuity of farmers and scientists and entrepreneurs to free this nation from the tyranny of oil once and for all.

141

One clear advantage Barack Obama had over Hillary Clinton, as far as most Democrats were concerned, was that he had opposed the Iraq War from the beginning. His speech of October 2002, calling it a "dumb war," had been widely distributed over the Internet. When Hillary Clinton tried to paint him as inexperienced, Obama could reply that good judgment was more important than many years of experience. In October 2002, Clinton had voted along with most of Congress to give President Bush the authority to attack Iraq.

In March, Barack Obama was hit with some bad publicity in connection with the Reverend Jeremiah Wright. Besides being Obama's friend and pastor for twenty years, Wright had a small role in Obama's campaign as one of more than 170 people on Obama's African-American Religious Leadership Committee. Now ABC News was broadcasting video clips of Wright's fiery sermons in which he had sharply criticized the United States for its racism. He had also said the United States had brought the disaster of September 11, 2001, on itself through its own "terrorism."

Most Americans were shocked and outraged by Wright's words, and they wondered how Barack Obama could be so close to Wright. Obama asked Wright to drop

142

his association with the campaign, since his presence could only hurt the candidate now. Obama also told the media that he strongly condemned Wright's inflammatory statements. But he didn't repudiate Wright. He felt that would be disloyal to the minister who had baptized him when he joined the church, married him and Michelle, and baptized their children.

The incident convinced Obama that he needed to talk openly to Americans, white and black, about the issue of race relations in the United States. He wrote a speech entitled "A More Perfect Union," a phrase from the preamble to the U.S. Constitution. To underline his belief that the fundamental principles of the nation were at stake, he gave the speech at the National Constitution Center in Philadelphia.

Obama said afterward that he was "channeling my mother" as he wrote the speech. He remembered her positive, practical approach to racial differences, and how disturbed she'd been by the anger that the black leader Malcolm X expressed in the 1960s. Perhaps he also remembered the story of the time his father won over the white man in the bar at Waikiki by talking to him about race in a straightforward, confident way.

143

Most media commentators and politicians, Republican as well as Democratic, praised Obama's courage in addressing the racial issue, and felt that he handled it well. Chris Matthews of MSNBC said Obama had given "what many of us think is one of the great speeches in American history." However, in the short run the uproar over Wright caused Obama's favorability in the polls to drop from 50 percent to 45 percent.

That might have been the end of the incident, except that in April, Jeremiah Wright appeared before the National Press Club and repeated his controversial views. Worse, he suggested that Obama secretly agreed with him. At this point Barack Obama finally felt forced to disown his former friend and pastor. In May, the Obamas reluctantly left Trinity Church.

In early March, in the Republican primaries, Senator John McCain had become the presumptive nominee—meaning that the party would formally nominate him during their national convention in September. McCain could afford to relax a bit and gather his forces for the general election, while Barack Obama and Hillary Clinton kept up a fierce struggle for the Democratic nomination through March, April, and May. But Obama gradually outdistanced Clinton.

On June 3, when all the primary results were in, Obama had enough delegates to win the Democratic nomination. He was now the presumptive nominee of the Democratic Party. On June 7, Clinton announced that she was endorsing Obama.

For the general election, Obama would need more money. In 2004 both George W. Bush's campaign and John Kerry's campaign had raised well over $200 million. Some political observers predicted that each major candidate in the 2008 election would have to raise more than $400 million.

In mid-June, Obama decided to turn down public financing for the general election. Public financing would provide $84 million, but then the candidate had to accept strict spending limits. Obama was confident that he could raise much more than $84 million, since he'd raised $55 million in February alone. This was a new record for fund-raising in one month. In order to challenge John McCain in traditionally Republican states, he would need large amounts of money, and he would need freedom from spending limits.

In June alone, the Obama campaign raised $52 million, more than twice the amount raised by John McCain.

Senator McCain had accepted public funding for the general election, and his campaign criticized Obama loudly for failing to "stand on principle and keep his word to the American people." This was a reminder that Obama had originally agreed to limit himself to public funding if his Republican opponent did the same.

During this year of nonstop campaigning, Barack Obama tried to weave his family life in with his hectic schedule. Since Barack was scheduled to give an Independence Day speech in Butte, Montana, Michelle decided that the Obamas would celebrate Malia's birthday while watching the Fourth of July parade there. So Barack gave his speech, and the Obamas hosted a picnic in Butte for family and friends. Malia would have a private birthday party with her friends the week after her actual birthday.

Also on Barack and Michelle's schedule during the Fourth of July celebration was an interview for the program *Access Hollywood*. They hadn't planned to include Malia and Sasha in the interview, but Barack and Michelle were in a relaxed mood that day and thought it might be fun. The interviewer was surprised and delighted to include the girls at the last minute.

Malia told the interviewer how her father had embarrassed her once by shaking hands with one of her nine-year-old friends, as if she were a voter. "You don't really shake hands with kids," explained Malia. Sasha confided that everyone in the family except her father liked ice cream. She and Malia agreed that their parents were most likely to get mad at them for whining. They also agreed that they liked to see their parents holding hands or kissing.

In all, the interview didn't reveal anything very private, and Michelle and the children didn't seem uncomfortable about it. But Barack said afterward that it was a mistake. "I don't think it's healthy and it's something that we'll be avoiding in the future," he said. His family life was very precious to him, and this felt a little too intrusive.

Ever since Barack Obama emerged as the likely Democratic candidate, Senator McCain had been attacking him for his lack of foreign policy experience. McCain had strongly supported the Iraq War from the beginning, and he tried to cast Obama as naïve and ignorant of military matters. McCain kept challenging Obama to travel to Iraq and see for himself how well the war was going.

Obama saw this challenge as an opportunity, and he was glad to take McCain up on it. By meeting with world leaders and visiting troubled parts of the world, he could demonstrate to American voters that he had a statesman-like presence. He could discuss his views about various important decisions he would have to make if he won the election. So later in July, Obama left for the Middle East and western Europe.

Obama asked Senators Chuck Hagel of Nebraska and Jack Reed of Rhode Island to travel to Iraq with him. Hagel, though Republican, had criticized the Bush admin-istration repeatedly for its conduct of the Iraq War. Also, as a member of the Senate Foreign Relations Committee, Hagel had experience that Obama lacked. Reed, a Demo-crat, was a member of the important Senate Armed Forces Committee. Reed had been in Congress since 1990, and Hagel since 1996.

One of the highlights of Obama's trip abroad was his stop in Berlin, Germany. There, at the Berlin Wall that had once separated Soviet-dominated East Germany from West Germany, he spoke to a crowd of 200,000, many of them waving American flags. Viewers remembered that President John F. Kennedy and President Ronald Reagan had also made memorable speeches in Berlin. If McCain intended to make his rival look presidential, he had succeeded.

CHAPTER 15

PRESIDENT BARACK OBAMA

THE DEMOCRATIC NATIONAL CONVENTION OF 2008 was held at the end of August in Denver, Colorado. It had already been decided that the convention would nominate Barack Obama for president. But it was vital for the Democrats to heal the split between the Obama camp and the Clinton camp. Many supporters of Hillary Clinton were bitterly disappointed, and some of them even threatened to vote for Republican John McCain.

Just before the convention began, Barack Obama announced his choice for vice president: Senator Joe Biden of Delaware. Senator Biden had served in the Senate since 1973, and he had extensive experience in foreign policy, which Obama lacked.

On August 25, the first day of the convention, Michelle Obama gave the headline prime-time speech. Republicans had often tried to portray her as a tough, almost radical woman—not the kind of person Americans would want as First Lady. Michelle took this chance to emphasize her traditional values and devotion to her family.

The following night Senator Hillary Clinton gave the headline prime-time speech, directing it chiefly to her supporters. She thanked them for fighting for her, but urged them to work just as hard for Barack Obama. In a pointed rejection of the idea that Clinton backers might now swing to Senator McCain, she said with great emphasis, "No way. No how. No McCain."

The following day Senator Clinton called for suspending the roll call of delegates and nominating Barack Obama by acclamation. That night, former president Bill Clinton further reinforced party unity by declaring, "Barack Obama is ready to be president of the United States."

For Barack Obama's acceptance speech on August 28, the convention moved to Invesco Field at Mile High Stadium in Denver. Nearly 80,000 people packed the stadium, and 38 million Americans watched the televised event. Speaking on the theme "Change You Can Believe In," Obama inspired the audience with hope for the future. "I will restore our moral standing," he promised, "so that

America is once again that last, best hope for all who are called to the cause of freedom, who long for lives of peace, and who yearn for a better future."

With the success of the convention, Obama's numbers rose in the polls. However, the very next day John McCain grabbed the nation's attention by announcing his choice for vice president. To the surprise of almost everyone, he picked Governor Sarah Palin of Alaska, who had no national political experience.

At the Republican National Convention in St. Paul, Minnesota, the following week, Republicans responded to Sarah Palin with enthusiasm. They liked her cheerfully feisty style, her working-class background, and her conservative beliefs. They were hopeful that many independent voters who had supported Senator Clinton would now be drawn to Governor Palin. Coming out of the convention, the Republicans had renewed energy and a larger bump in the polls than expected.

Some Democrats were seriously worried that McCain might have gained a permanent advantage by choosing Palin. They begged Barack Obama to get angry at accusations from the McCain campaign they felt were unfair and to go on the attack. However, Obama refused to get rattled.

Meanwhile, the U.S. economy was shaken by the worst financial crisis since the Wall Street Crash in 1929, which had set off the Great Depression. The crisis had been building since 2007, when the housing bubble burst. The prices of private homes, which had been rising steadily for a number of years, fell sharply. Homeowners who had taken out large mortgages, expecting their houses to increase in value, were left with property worth less than the loans they had to pay back. Many of them simply could not make their payments, and hundreds of thousands of families faced losing their homes through foreclosure.

To make matters worse, many lenders had given mortgages to buyers who obviously could not afford them. These lenders had quickly sold the risky loans to investors, who now held worthless stock. During 2008, it came out that even respected and apparently solid financial institutions had invested heavily in the unsound mortgages.

The nation was shocked as some of the largest investment banks, including Bear Stearns and Lehman Brothers, collapsed. In rapid succession, other major financial institutions either went bankrupt or had to be bailed out by the federal government. In September, the government took over Fannie Mae and Freddie Mac, the largest mortgage-backing enterprises in the United States. Likewise, the government also took over the failing American International Group (AIG), an insurance giant.

On September 19, Secretary of the Treasury Henry M. Paulson Jr., speaking for the Bush administration, announced a rescue plan for the nation's entire financial system. Paulson asked Congress for the authority to buy up the unsound mortgage-backed securities that had caused the panic—as much as $700 billion worth.

The panic on the stock market was calmed for the moment by the news of a plan, but Congress was thrown into turmoil. Ordinary American citizens on "Main Street," struggling with rising prices, unemployment, and lack of health insurance, were outraged. As they told their representatives and senators, they did not want to bail out the "fat cats" on Wall Street who had invested recklessly and raked in big profits.

However, over the next week it became clear that the collapse of the U.S. banking system would cause disaster to ordinary Americans too. If banks failed, businesses would no longer be able to get the credit they needed to operate, and their employees would lose their jobs. Individuals would not be able to get loans to buy a car or send a child to college. The nation's economy would grind almost to a halt, as it had during the Great Depression.

Congress discussed frantically how to act on Paulson's proposal. John McCain announced that he was suspending his campaign until the financial crisis was solved. He called for the first presidential debate, scheduled for September 26, to be postponed.

Remaining calm, Barack Obama consulted with a group of economic experts, conservative as well as liberal. He had believed for some time that speculation in the home mortgage market was a serious threat to the nation's economic health.

On September 26, although Congress was still working out an agreement, Senator McCain flew from Washington to Mississippi for the presidential debate. The location, the University of Mississippi in Oxford, underlined the historic significance of Barack Obama's candidacy. The university, known as "Ole Miss," had been the scene of race riots in 1962, when the first black student, James Meredith, attempted to enroll.

During the debate John McCain tried to cast Barack Obama as inexperienced and naïve about foreign policy and military issues. Obama repeatedly linked McCain to the failures of the eight-year Bush administration. Obama also pointed out that Senator McCain, in spite of his years of experience, had been wrong on several crucial issues. Obama reminded the audience that the war in Iraq, which Senator McCain had predicted would be won easily, was draining $10 billion per month from the U.S. Treasury.

Obama also emphasized that Senator McCain had supported President Bush's economic policies, including the decision to loosen government regulation of banks. Obama quoted McCain as declaring recently that "the fundamentals of our economy are strong." Given the desperate condition of the U.S. economy, that made McCain seem hopelessly out of touch.

While neither man clearly won or lost the debate, polls a week later showed that Obama was in the lead again. Voters saw him as more capable than McCain of handling the financial crisis, which was their top concern. And some of the enthusiasm for McCain's running mate, Sarah Palin, had worn off.

On September 29, the House of Representatives defeated a measure based on the Bush administration's plan for rescuing the financial system. The Dow Jones industrial average, a main indicator of the stock market, promptly dropped more than 770 points, its biggest one-day loss ever. It was obvious that Congress had to act, no matter how unpopular the rescue measure was with their constituents. On October 3, the House passed a revised version of the bill, already approved by the Senate.

With up to $700 billion now committed to the financial rescue plan, Barack Obama knew as president he would not be able to accomplish all the goals that he envisioned. Still, Obama was determined to give tax relief to middle-class and working-class citizens, and to reform the health-care system so that all Americans had adequate health care. He was also resolved to invest in programs that would create thousands of jobs at the same time that they benefited the country in other ways. One was an energy program for developing renewable sources of energy and ending dependence on foreign oil. Another was a plan to repair the nation's run-down roadways and bridges.

The second presidential debate took place on October 7 at Belmont University in Nashville, Tennessee. The format of this debate was town-hall style. More than eighty undecided voters shared the stage with the two candidates and the moderator. Barack Obama and John McCain answered questions from the undecided voters, as well as questions sent in by e-mail. Most of the questions dealt with the faltering economy, which had lost 159,000 jobs in September.

In a poll taken immediately after the debate, voters' opinion of McCain didn't change, but their opinion of Obama rose by a few points. Republican as well as Democratic commentators agreed that Obama had won the debate by a slight margin. But the race was still too close to call. The third and last debate was held on October 15, at Hofstra University in Hempstead, New York.

During the third debate Senator McCain attacked Obama more vigorously, but Obama remained calm and cool. He kept the focus on the faltering national economy, which he blamed on the Bush administration's policies, and repeated his claim that a McCain presidency would be like having four more years of George W. Bush. The economy was still by far the main issue for voters, and it appeared they had more confidence in Obama's ability to lead the country out of the economic crisis. National polls showed Obama ahead. In the final week, Obama's lead narrowed, but most national polls still put him ahead.

In the last stretch of the campaign, many moderate Republicans came out in support of Barack Obama.

Colin Powell, the greatly respected former general and former secretary of state in the Bush administration, endorsed Obama. So did former Massachusetts governor William Weld.

This had been a watershed race for the presidency in several ways. For one thing, Hillary Clinton was the first woman to come so close to winning a major party nomination. Sarah Palin was the first woman to be nominated for vice president by the Republican party. John McCain, if he had won the election, would have been the oldest president to begin a first term. But most striking, Barack Obama was the first African–American candidate nominated by a major party. If he won, it would signal an important change in Americans' attitudes toward race.

The presidential contest of 2008 had been the longest as well as the most expensive campaign in U.S. history, costing more than $1 billion total. The McCain campaign spent $176 million just on television advertising, while the Obama campaign spent $278 million. The Obama campaign had received a record number of more than three million donations, large and small; Obama could afford to advertise even in states where he wasn't likely to win, such as Senator McCain's home state of Arizona. Besides

money, Obama had the advantage of a huge army of volunteers to go door to door in the battleground states, such
as Ohio, to get out the vote.

Although both McCain and Obama had set out to
wage positive campaigns, the election turned negative in
the final weeks. Senator McCain had told his team not to
bring up the subject of Obama's former pastor, the controversial Jeremiah Wright. However, at the end of October
the National Republican Trust PAC ran television advertisements in Ohio, Pennsylvania, and Florida reminding
voters of Obama's close association with Wright. As for
the Obama team, they gleefully publicized Vice President
Richard Cheney's endorsement of John McCain. They
had worked for many months to link Senator McCain
with the unpopular Bush administration, and Vice President Cheney was even less popular than the president.

The presidential election of 2008 promised to be a
record-setter for voter turnout. Since a low in the election
of 1996, the turnout for presidential elections had been
slowly rising. In 2008, both Democrats and Republicans
made extra efforts to register voters and get them to the
polls. There were predictions that the turnout would top
the 63.1 percent of 1960, when John F. Kennedy won the

presidency. It might even match the 66 percent of a century ago in 1908, when William Howard Taft was elected president. The Democrats had registered an unusually large number of new black, Hispanic, and young voters, groups with typically low turnout rates. All these groups tended to favor Barack Obama.

During the hectic last weeks of the campaign, Barack Obama took a trip to Hawaii. His grandmother Madelyn Dunham, eighty-six, was gravely ill, and it was not certain that she would live even until Election Day. However, she was mentally alert, and Obama was glad he could spend time at her bedside, talking with her. Michelle, campaigning in place of her husband, told the audience what Barack's grandmother had meant to him. "She taught him with her quiet confidence and love and support that he could do anything."

Barack's sister Maya was with their grandmother when she died on November 3. Although it was sad that Madelyn Dunham hadn't lived long enough to see her grandson elected president, she had been able to vote for him by absentee ballot. And by the day before the election, it seemed probable that Obama would be the winner.

Obama had held up well under the long, high-pressure

campaign, although he looked older than he had when it had begun almost two years before. There was gray in his hair, and he had lost some weight. But he was steadier and more confident than ever. His steadiness was reflected in the tireless, well-organized work of his campaign, and his calm, resolute manner had convinced voters that Obama had the right temperament for the stressful job of president of the United States. On Wednesday, October 29, more than 33 million viewers watched a thirty-minute "infomercial" aired during prime time on the major networks by the Obama campaign. The advertisement combined images from the campaign trail with clips of Barack Obama addressing voters, as well as of ordinary Americans telling about their difficulties in these hard economic times.

On November 3, Barack Obama made a last push to win the battleground states. He began the day with a rally in Jacksonville, Florida. He traveled on to rallies in North Carolina and Virginia. If Barack Obama won all the states the polls showed as leaning Democratic, as well as the solidly Democratic states, he would have 291 electoral votes—more than the 270 he needed to win. But he and his followers were not going to relax at this point. They aimed for a wide margin of victory, which would help unite the country behind the new president.

On the evening of November 3, Obama appeared in a prerecorded interview on the TV program *Monday Night Football.* Asked about the best advice he'd ever gotten from the sports world, Obama remembered the words of his high school basketball coach, who told him, "This is not about you. It's about the team." Obama gave a related answer to another question: What personality quality of his did he want voters to think about as they went to the polls? He said, "That I'm going to fight for them."

On November 4, Election Day, Barack and Michelle Obama, accompanied by Malia and Sasha, voted at a neighborhood elementary school. The girls hoped their father would win, of course. But in any case, they were happy the long campaign was almost over. Their parents had promised them a puppy after the election. Afterward, Barack was off to Indianapolis for a final campaign stop.

That afternoon, Obama returned to Chicago to await the election returns. He followed his Election Day tradition of playing basketball with friends, then ate dinner at home with his family. His election night rally was scheduled to begin at eight thirty Central time at Grant Park in

Chicago, a site which could hold hundreds of thousands of people. Everyone at the rally would have to stand for several hours.

Polling officials had been worried that the large turn-out would cause problems at voting sites, and in some places voters did have to wait in line for hours. But that year many more voters—almost a third—cast their votes early, as most states allowed early or no-excuse absentee ballot voting. Apparently the unusual number of early voters helped prevent congestion at the polls on Election Day itself.

The TV networks were cautious about calling the election too early, because in 2004 some of them had mistakenly reported John Kerry in the lead, based on unreliable exit polls. This year, they agreed not to call the results for a state until all the votes for that state were in.

As polls in the Eastern time zone began to close, the country watched especially for results from the contested states of Indiana, Virginia, North Carolina, Florida, and New Hampshire. If Obama won these, it would be a clear signal that the election was going his way.

Pennsylvania was also important, because John McCain had fought long and hard to win this Democratic-leaning state. If he did win Pennsylvania, it would be an encouraging sign that he might win the election after all. But Pennsylvania went for Obama. Ohio, too, was a key battleground state. No Republican in modern times had won the presidency without Ohio—and Ohio went for Barack Obama.

Before eleven p.m. Eastern time, it was clear that Obama would also win Virginia. At eleven, when the polls closed on the West Coast and Obama carried California, Washington, and Oregon, most of the networks pronounced Barack Obama the winner. The final results would not be reported until the following day, but already Obama had more than 300 electoral votes. It would be a sweeping victory. John McCain called Obama from Phoenix, Arizona, to concede the election.

All across the country, the rallies for Obama turned into celebration parties. At midnight, Barack Obama appeared on the stage in front of the enormous crowd at Grant Park to give his victory speech. Thanking all his supporters, he told them that the victory truly belonged to them, rather than him. He called for all Americans to unite to solve the serious problems facing the country.

President-elect Obama told an inspiring story of one voter in Atlanta: Ann Nixon Cooper, an African-American woman who was 106 years old. "She was born just a genera-tion past slavery; a time when there were no cars on the road or planes in the sky; when someone like her couldn't vote for two reasons—because she was a woman and because ot the color of her skin.

"And tonight, I think about all that she's seen through-out her century in America—the heartache and the hope; the struggle and the progress; the times we were told that we can't, and the people who pressed on with that Ameri-can creed: Yes, we can."

As Barack Obama continued his speech, he repeated again and again the phrase that had been the rallying cry of his campaign: "Yes, we can." And his audience, waving a sea of American flags, repeated solemnly, many with tears in their eyes, "Yes, we can."

"America," Obama finished, "we have come so far. We have seen so much. But there is so much more to do. So tonight, let us ask ourselves: If our children should live to see the next century—if my daughters should be so lucky to live as long as Ann Nixon Cooper—what change will they see? What progress will we have made?

"This is our chance to answer that call. This is our moment. This is our time—to put our people back to work and open doors of opportunity for our kids; to restore prosperity and promote the cause of peace; to reclaim the American Dream and reaffirm that fundamental truth— that out of many, we are one; that while we breathe, we hope; and where we are met with cynicism, and doubt, and those who tell us that we can't, we will respond with that timeless creed that sums up the spirit of a people: Yes, we can."

CHAPTER 16

A NEW START

ON JANUARY 20, 2009, BARACK OBAMA STOOD ON the steps of the Capitol to be sworn in as the forty-fourth president. As he took the oath, he rested his hand on the same Bible that Abraham Lincoln had used on Inauguration Day in 1861. Later, Obama would place Lincoln's bust in the Oval Office, along with that of another of his heroes, Dr. Martin Luther King Jr.

Inauguration Day was icy, with a windchill of 17 degrees Farenheit. But the crowds on the Capitol grounds and the National Mall were the largest audience for any event ever held in Washington, D.C. All over the world, on TV and live video streams, many more millions of people watched the inauguration of the first African-American president of the United States.

The mood of the crowd in Washington was joyful, but

the new president struck a sober tone in his inauguration speech. After all, the country was fighting wars in both Iraq and Afghanistan, and struggling with the worst economic crisis since the Great Depression. President Obama talked about the "new era of responsibility" in American life—responsibility for both government and ordinary people to cope with the serious challenges ahead. After he finished speaking, his daughter Sasha told him, "That was a pretty good speech, Dad."

After the ceremonies and the inaugural balls and parties were over, the new president got down to work. Even before his election, Barack Obama had been thinking hard about the people he would appoint to head the various departments of the executive branch of the federal government. They would be his cabinet, his official group of advisers.

Secretary of state, the person who would be in charge of the United States' relations with other countries, was an especially important cabinet post. Obama chose Hillary Clinton, who had been his chief rival for the Democratic nomination. He thought she was the most able person for the job, and he also thought that having her on his team would heal a rift in the Democratic Party.

For secretary of defense, another key role, President

Obama decided to keep Robert Gates, from George W. Bush's administration, in the position. Gates was experienced, and he agreed with Obama's plans to withdraw from Iraq. Furthermore, Obama intended this appointment as a signal to Republicans that the new Democratic president genuinely wanted to work with them.

For secretary of the treasury, Obama chose Timothy Geithner. As chairman of the Federal Reserve Bank of New York, Geithner had a deep understanding of the country's financial crisis. He had also helped prevent a meltdown of the U.S. financial system in 2008, although he had been bitterly criticized for not getting the government better leverage over the banks in return.

President Obama's choice for ambassador to the United Nations was Susan E. Rice, assistant secretary of state for African affairs in the Clinton administration. The post of UN ambassador was not part of the cabinet, but many presidents, Republicans as well as Democrats, had given the position cabinet-level rank. However, President George W. Bush had dropped it to a lower level. Now President Obama emphasized the respect he had for the United Nations by raising the ambassadorship to cabinet rank again.

Besides his cabinet, President Obama had many posi-
tions to fill during his first year. One of the most important was a vacancy on the Supreme Court. He chose Sonia
Sotomayor, a judge on the U.S. Court of Appeals for the
Second Circuit in New York. She was the first Hispanic to
be appointed to the highest court in the land.

Immediately after taking office, the new president was
able to keep some of his campaign promises by issuing
executive orders. Many of these reversed policies from the
George W. Bush administration. For instance, Guantánamo
Bay, a prison at the U.S. naval base in Cuba where the Bush
administration housed suspected terrorists, had become a
worldwide symbol of harsh and unjust treatment by the
United States. President Obama ordered Guantánamo
closed. Likewise, he ended the Bush policy of "enhanced
interrogation" of enemy prisoners, including techniques
condemned by the UN Committee against Torture. And
he ordered a policy of greater openness with presidential
records.

President Obama also set a timetable for withdrawing
U.S. troops from Iraq. He ended "stop-loss," the practice of
keeping soldiers on active service beyond their expected
tour of duty, and in 2011, he ordered an end to "Don't ask,

don't tell," a policy that discriminated against homosexuals in the military.

In the areas of health and science, President Obama loosened federal restrictions on embryonic stem-cell research. He removed President George W. Bush's ban on federal funding to overseas health organizations that included abortion in their family-planning programs. And he signed the Children's Health Insurance Program Reauthorization Act of 2009, providing health insurance to millions more children and women throughout the states.

Significantly, the *very* first legislation that President Obama signed was the Lilly Ledbetter Fair Pay Act of 2009. His immediate action underlined how important he considered equal pay for women.

However, among all the problems clamoring for attention as Barack Obama began his presidency, the most urgent was the U.S. economy. It was still on the edge of collapse. The Bush administration had rescued some key financial institutions during the fall of 2008, but the economy was caught in a vicious downward cycle.

The American economy was losing about 200,000 jobs a month. As people lost their paychecks, they became unable to pay their mortgages, and the banks foreclosed on their homes. The housing market, so important to the U.S. economy, dwindled even further. And as the unemployed spent less and less money, even on food and clothing, many businesses were forced to cut back or even close. As a result, still more workers lost their jobs.

Long before Inauguration Day, President-elect Obama and his advisers had been consulting with congressional leaders on how to keep the country from plunging into a second Great Depression. In January 2009, Congress began debating the American Recovery and Reinvestment Act. This plan, also called the "stimulus package," was intended to give the U.S. economy a massive boost.

The American Recovery and Reinvestment Act (ARRA) provided for $787 billion in federal aid. To ease some of the worst suffering in the country, it gave the states money to expand unemployment benefits and food stamp programs. The Recovery Act also gave income tax credits to Americans who were working but still poor. The president and his advisers hoped that people who received tax credits, unemployment checks, and food stamps would spend this money right away, helping to break the economy's downward cycle.

The stimulus plan also provided money for the maintenance of crumbling infrastructure, such as highways and bridges; development of alternative energy sources; and investment in education. Some of the stimulus money would allow struggling state and local governments to keep employees such as teachers and firefighters. These measures would save or create badly needed jobs, and help the economy move away from financial and real-estate speculation.

Conservatives in Congress objected strongly to the cost of the stimulus, which was even more than President Franklin Roosevelt had spent in the first months of 1933 to combat the Great Depression when adjusted for inflation. They argued that since the United States was already deep in debt, the country could not afford to spend more. Also, they believed that the best way to stimulate the economy was to cut taxes and remove regulations on businesses, so they could grow and hire more workers.

Some provisions favored by conservatives were added to the final bill, but even so, not a single Republican in the House, and only three in the Senate, voted for it. However, the Democratic majority in Congress passed the stimulus package. On February 17, 2009, Obama signed the bill into law.

In the fall of 2008, the Bush administration had taken emergency measures to keep the national banking system from breaking down. Congress passed the Troubled Asset Relief Program (TARP), providing $700 billion to bail out the major banks. President Obama continued these measures and also provided $17.4 billion to General Motors and Chrysler, preventing the automobile industry from collapsing. In exchange for receiving federal aid, the president required the auto companies to restructure, and forced them to adopt stricter fuel economy standards.

These actions were unpopular with many American voters. They were angry at the federal government for rescuing investment bankers and the heads of automobile corporations, while average Americans lost their jobs and their homes. They wanted the big banks and corporations punished, not helped.

But President Obama and his economic advisers were sure that letting the banks and automobile manufacturers fail would cause even more suffering for ordinary Americans. More than one and a half million jobs depended on the "Big Three" automakers—General Motors, Chrysler LLC, and Ford Motor. That included not only people working at the automakers themselves, but also people employed by auto dealers or auto parts suppliers.

The president believed the bailouts were necessary in the short run. But what would help the economy the most in the long run, he thought, was health-care reform. In addition, improved health care would make a tremendous difference in the lives of average Americans.

The public/private health-care system in the United States was the most expensive in the world, but it was far from the best. In a World Health Organization report, the U.S. actually ranked *last* among nine wealthy nations in two important measures: infant mortality (what proportion of babies died in their first year of life) and life expectancy (how many years the average person could expect to live).

More than forty million Americans had no health insurance, and in the economic downturn, more and more of them were losing the insurance connected with their jobs. Insurance companies could refuse to insure people who already had medical problems, and sometimes they also dropped customers when they became ill. Even insured Americans often went bankrupt from the expense of serious illness.

Presidents over the years, beginning with Republican

Theodore Roosevelt, had seen the need to control health-care costs and offer health care to all Americans. However, none of them had been able to persuade Congress to enact such policies. The last Democratic president, Bill Clinton, had spent a great deal of time and energy trying to reform health care without any success.

As a candidate for president, Barack Obama had promised "to make health care affordable and available for every single American." He envisioned a law that would cover all uninsured Americans, limit the cost of health insurance, and allow workers to keep their insurance when they left a company. All Americans, he proposed, would be required to have health insurance.

But after he was elected, many in President Obama's administration tried to persuade him not to attempt health-care reform right away. They feared that the administration would get bogged down in this enormous task and not be able to accomplish anything else. Still, Obama was determined to push for health-care overhaul in his first year. If he didn't, he believed, the country would lose any chance of reforming the system for many years.

One of the most powerful champions of health-care reform was Senator Edward Kennedy of Massachusetts.

He had battled for this cause over the course of his long political career. Although diagnosed with a malignant brain tumor in 2008, Senator Kennedy kept his seat in the Senate through the summer of 2009, and did his best to guide the health-care reform bill through Congress. When Kennedy died in August 2009, the Obama administration lost a powerful ally. Still, in September 2009, Democratic leaders in the House of Representatives introduced the Patient Protection and Affordable Care Act.

During the summer and fall of 2009, the health-care reform bill was fiercely debated in Congress and in the media. Also, insurance companies, concerned that health-care reform would restrict their business, lobbied against it.

In the end, President Obama was forced to compromise on some features of the health-care bill. However, by March 2010, both houses of Congress had passed the amended bill, and on March 23, Obama signed it into law. Barack Obama had accomplished what no other president had been able to do in almost a century.

Americans were unsure about whether or not they liked the law. Some thought it allowed too much government interference with health care, while others felt it didn't achieve enough reform. But at least one part of health-care reform *was* popular. The new law allowed families to include children up to the age of twenty-six on their health insurance. As a result, a million more young adults now had coverage.

In foreign policy, the most pressing issues for President Obama were the wars in Iraq and Afghanistan. By early 2009, the Iraq War had cost the United States $612 billion. Thousands of U.S. soldiers had died, and thousands more had been seriously wounded. Also, the war had hurt America's reputation around the world, especially in Muslim nations. President Obama was determined to hand the responsibility for Iraq over to the Iraqis, and to withdraw U.S. troops from the country.

As for Afghanistan, President Obama believed that the United States had neglected its mission there: to destroy the terrorist organization that had attacked the U.S. on September 11, 2001. Before the end of that year, the U.S. had driven the Taliban, a fundamentalist Islamic regime that supported and protected al-Qaeda, from power. But since then, the Taliban had rebounded, and they relentlessly harassed American forces and the U.S.-backed government of President Hamid Karzai. Osama bin Laden, the head of al-Qaeda, was still at large.

In December 2009, President Obama announced that the United States would send 30,000 more troops to Afghanistan in a surge. The idea was to end the war quickly and decisively. Obama promised that within a few years, U.S. troops would be able to withdraw completely from the country.

In spite of these two wars in the Middle East, President Obama wanted to improve U.S. relations with Muslim nations. He was off to a good start—many people around the world felt more favorable toward the U.S. simply because an African-American with an Arabic-African name had been elected president. In his inauguration speech, Obama told Muslim countries, "We seek a new way forward, based on mutual interests and mutual respect." As the new president, he granted his first interview to Al Arabiya, a moderate Arabic-language TV channel. In June 2009, he traveled to Cairo, Egypt, to give a speech on American-Muslim relations.

Another issue that the new president wanted to address was the existence of large stockpiles of nuclear weapons left over from the Cold War. Barack Obama had made some progress on this problem as a senator, working with others to sponsor legislation aimed at reducing these stockpiles, but the United States and Russia still had dangerously large numbers of nuclear arms. In April 2009, President Obama met with the Russian president, Dmitry Medvedev, to kick off the drafting of a new Strategic Arms Reduction Treaty (START).

Still another worldwide threat was climate change, causing increased water shortages, droughts, flooding, and violent storms. President Obama was already encouraging the growth of clean-energy industries and raising fuel economy standards in the United States. In December 2009, he met with other world leaders at a conference in Copenhagen. The conference was disappointing in that it did not result in a legally binding treaty. But a nonbinding accord was signed by the U.S. and China, the world's two biggest carbon polluters, as well as by several other nations.

In October 2009, President Obama was awarded a great honor: the Nobel Peace Prize. The Norwegian Nobel Committee was honoring his efforts to reach out to the Muslim world, his respect for the United Nations, and his work to reduce stockpiles of nuclear weapons. In his acceptance speech, the president commented that many others deserved the prize more than he did. He also somberly pointed out that he was commander in chief of a nation in the middle of two wars.

Meanwhile, back in the United States, some of the Americans who had been most excited about Barack Obama's election were disappointed in the way he governed. They wanted an exciting, charismatic leader, but Obama made his decisions calmly and thoughtfully after long discussions with his advisers. He expected the people in his administration to work the same way. "No Drama Obama," his staff called him.

However, many Democrats missed the inspiring speeches of the campaign of 2008. In public appearances, the president's calm confidence sometimes gave the impression that he didn't care enough. Obama believed he could best reach his goals through reasonable discussion and compromise with the conservatives in Congress. But a growing number of his supporters wished he would fight his Republican opponents instead.

In spite of the enormous pressures of Barack Obama's job, his life as president was more relaxed than when he was campaigning. After almost two years on the road, he was glad to live and work in the same place. He joked about the advantages of "living over the store," as if the White House were a mom-and-pop grocery. For the first time in years, Barack and Michelle were able to eat dinner with Malia and Sasha most of the time.

Marian Robinson, Michelle's mother, moved into the White House with the family. Malia and Sasha started classes at Sidwell Friends School, which several White House children before them had attended. At home, the girls were expected to make their own beds and do other chores, even though the White House had a large staff to serve the president and his family.

Meanwhile, the girls wanted President Obama to fulfill his campaign promise to *them*: to get a puppy. Since Malia was allergic, the dog needed to be one with a nonshedding coat, such as a poodle or a Portuguese water dog. Senator Edward Kennedy, who loved Portuguese water dogs, offered the First Family a Portie puppy. In April 2009, the six-month-old dog with a curly, black coat, white front paws, and a white bib arrived at the White House. Malia and Sasha named him Bo.

Meanwhile, Michelle Obama, eager to use her position as First Lady to promote healthy eating, broke ground for a White House vegetable garden. And President Obama had basketball hoops installed on the White House tennis courts. He often hosted pickup games with friends and fellow politicians, as well as professional athletes.

CHAPTER 17

SLOW PROGRESS

WHEN BARACK OBAMA WAS FIRST ELECTED PRESI-
dent, there was widespread hope that this could be the
beginning of a new era of cooperation in American politics.
Obama had won the popular vote by a solid margin, 52.7
percent to John McCain's 45.7 percent, and the Democrats
were in the majority in both the House and the Senate. But
he expected to work out compromises with the Republicans in Congress rather than force his policies upon them.

However, Republican opposition to anything President Obama proposed was fierce. Beginning early in
2009, Republicans fought hard against his stimulus package, although it included large tax cuts and many conces-
sions to their demands. The bill passed with only three
Republicans in Congress voting for it. When the president
presented his health-care reform bill to a joint session of

Congress in September 2009, a Republican congressman from South Carolina interrupted him, shouting, "You lie!" No member of Congress had ever done such a thing to a president, and even most Republicans were shocked.

Still, during the next several months, President Obama worked hard to cooperate with his opponents and get the bill enacted into law. Many Democrats were angry that he compromised so much, and when it came time to vote on the Patient Protection and Affordable Care Act, every Republican in both the House and the Senate voted against it. Immediately after the president signed the bill into law, Republicans began efforts to repeal it.

In October 2010, shortly before midterm elections for many congressional seats, the Senate minority leader, Republican Mitch McConnell, stated, "The single most important thing we want to achieve is for President Obama to be a one-term president." As a means of working toward that goal, Republicans hoped to deny President Obama any successes. If they could repeal his major achievement, the Patient Protection and Affordable Care Act, and prevent him from pulling the country out of recession, they could make him look like a weak president.

Outside of Washington, wild rumors about Barack

Obama circulated on the Internet and were spread by radio and TV talk show hosts. One was that he was secretly a Muslim. This was based on the fact that Obama's father had been raised in Kenya as a Muslim, and that Obama had been named after his father with the Arab names "Barack" and "Hussein." Also, Obama had lived in Indonesia, a majority Muslim country, from age six to age ten. However, his Indonesian stepfather was not a devout Muslim, his mother did not belong to any organized religion, and the public school Barack attended in Indonesia did not promote any religion.

As an adult, Barack Obama had not practiced a religion until he moved to Chicago and worked as a community organizer. There he was baptized as a Christian and joined the Trinity United Church of Christ. Since becoming president, Obama's main place of worship has been the Evergreen Chapel at Camp David, the First Family's country retreat.

Another persistent rumor was that Barack Obama had actually been born in Kenya, rather than the United States. If this were true, he would not be a natural-born U.S. citizen. Therefore, according to the Constitution, he could not serve as president.

But such rumors were ridiculous, for anyone who wanted to could check the facts. Ann Dunham Sutoro, Obama's mother, had never traveled outside the United States until six years after her son was born. In 2008, the Hawaii's Department of Health formally certified that Barack Hussein Obama Jr. had been born at Kapi'olani Medical Center in Honolulu.

Still, the "birthers" continued to repeat the rumors so loudly and so often that more than one fifth of Americans doubted that the president had been born in the U.S. In April 2011, Barack Obama decided to release the official long form of his birth certificate to the public. "We do not have time for this kind of silliness," he told reporters at a press conference. "We've got better stuff to do."

A good example of the "better stuff" was ending the United States' dependence on foreign oil. In the past, the quest for oil had drawn the U.S. into alliances with some unsavory dictators and prompted ill-advised military actions. President Obama preferred to achieve energy independence through renewable sources, such as wind power and solar power, but he also acknowledged the need to find more oil in the United States.

In March 2009, the president allowed a limited amount

of deepwater oil drilling in the Gulf of Mexico. President Obama judged that the benefit of new oil sources within the United States was worth the risk of pollution. Also, he hoped that Republicans, who favored offshore drilling, would now be more likely to go along with his proposals for developing clean-energy sources and slowing down climate change.

Republicans tended to go along with the many Americans who scoffed at the threat of global warming. Although the majority of the scientific community agreed that climate change was taking place and had the potential to wreak havoc on the world, nearly half the American population thought that the dangers of climate change had been exaggerated. Furthermore, they did not believe that human activities had much impact on the global climate.

On April 20, 2010, an offshore oil rig in the Gulf of Mexico exploded, killing eleven workers. Oil gushed uncontrolled from the well into the sea at an estimated rate of over 53,000 barrels a day. The operator of the rig, the international energy company BP, worked frantically to cap the spill. But in spite of their efforts, the oil continued to flow for the next three months.

There was widespread damage to wildlife and the

environment, and the fishing and tourist industries in the Gulf were badly hurt. Almost 500 miles of coastline in four states was contaminated by the spill. This was the largest offshore oil spill in U.S. history.

After investigation, the Obama administration concluded that BP had skimped on safety measures to cut costs. Some people blamed President Obama for allowing any drilling off the Gulf Coast. In December, he halted offshore drilling on the entire East Coast and the eastern Gulf of Mexico.

In foreign policy, President Obama made progress toward ending the long and costly war in Iraq. After a steady withdrawal of U.S. troops, President Obama announced in August 2010 that the seven-year U.S. combat mission in Iraq had concluded. Some U.S. troops remained in the country to train and advise Iraqi troops, but by the end of 2011, all U.S. troops would be gone. This would allow the United States to focus its military strength on Afghanistan, the country from which the terrorist organization al-Qaeda had attacked the U.S. on September 11, 2001.

One of the most frustrating things about the war in Afghanistan was that Osama bin Laden, head of al-Qaeda, was still at large. Then during 2010, the Central Intelligence Agency (CIA) learned that he was hiding in Pakistan, near the capital city of Islamabad. On May 1, 2011, President Obama ordered the U.S. Navy SEALs to raid bin Laden's compound. Osama bin Laden himself was killed in the raid.

Otherwise, progress in Afghanistan had been disappointing. The elected government of President Hamid Karzai was weak and corrupt, and the Taliban insurgency threatened to overwhelm them. But the American public was tired of this costly war, which had now dragged on for longer than any other American war. In June 2011, President Obama announced a schedule to gradually withdraw U.S. combat troops from Afghanistan, finishing by 2014.

Elsewhere in the Middle East, protests against repressive governments broke out in several countries at the end of 2010 and the beginning of 2011. One of these countries was Libya, ruled for over forty years by the brutal dictator Muammar Gaddafi. President Obama wanted to support the pro-democracy movement and prevent Gaddafi from massacring his own people. But to avoid the appearance that the United States was invading yet another Muslim country, he waited for the UN to pass a resolution allowing member nations to establish a no-fly zone in Libya.

Once that happened, the president immediately ordered air strikes on Gaddafi's air defense, but then he let France and Britain take the lead in a combined North Atlantic Treaty Organization (NATO) no-fly force. In October 2011, the Libyan rebels took over the country and killed Gaddafi.

One goal President Obama thought he had already accomplished early in 2009 was the closing of the infamous Guantánamo detention camp. But the Senate voted to block the funds necessary to transfer or release prisoners and close the camp. Additionally, nearly all of the senators, Democrats as well as Republicans, voted not to allow any prisoners—even ones who had been detained by mistake—to be transferred to the United States. In 2011, Obama decided to drop the issue of Guantánamo for the time being and concentrate on solving other problems.

One such problem had been growing since Barack Obama's first year as president. It was a movement calling itself the "Tea Party." The Americans in this movement, mainly conservative Republicans, believed that taxes were too high, and that the government spent too much and interfered too much in the lives of its citizens. At rallies, they wore three-cornered hats in the style of Thomas

Jefferson and George Washington, symbolizing their feeling that the United States had drifted from the original vision of the men who founded the country. Tea Partiers opposed President Obama and most of his policies, and they threw their support behind conservative politicians.

In the elections of 2010, the Democrats lost sixty-three seats in the House of Representatives. President Obama ruefully called the elections a "shellacking" of his party. The Democrats were no longer the majority, and John Boehner, Republican, replaced Nancy Pelosi, Democrat, in the powerful position of Speaker of the House. Many of the new Republican representatives were allied with the Tea Party movement.

The Senate still had a Democratic majority, but the rules of the Senate made it easy for a determined minority to block legislation. Scott Brown, Republican from Massachusetts, had already been elected to take the seat formerly held by Obama's ally Senator Ted Kennedy. Now it would be even more difficult for the president to persuade Congress to pass any given bill.

By coincidence, a few weeks later, Barack Obama got elbowed in the face during one of his pickup basketball games. It wasn't a serious injury, but he needed stitches in his upper lip. To the public, the president's swollen lip looked like a visible sign of the beating his party had taken in the elections.

With their new strength, Republicans hoped to block or overturn more of the legislation that President Obama had managed to enact. And if they couldn't repeal the president's measures, they would attempt to deny them funding. A big target was the health-care reform in the Patient Protection and Affordable Care Act. They were working to have the Supreme Court declare the act unconstitutional.

In addition, the Republicans in Congress were more determined than ever not to compromise with the Democrats. The influential Tea Party group was especially opposed to new taxes in any form. In fact, they believed that the only road back to prosperity for the United States was to reduce taxes, especially on businesses and investors, and cut federal spending. They thought the first priority should be paying down the federal deficit, the amount of money owed by the United States to other countries.

President Obama, too, was concerned about the U.S. budget deficit. During the eight years of the George W. Bush administration, the U.S. budget surplus achieved under the Clinton administration had disappeared, and the deficit had ballooned to $485 billion. Still, Obama believed that getting unemployed Americans back to work was more urgent than reducing the deficit. And in the long run, the way to reduce the deficit was to first make the U.S. prosperous again.

At the beginning of 2011, Treasury Secretary Timothy Geithner announced that the federal government did not have enough money to pay its obligations—the spending that Congress had already voted for. Because of big tax cuts during the Bush years, and because so many Americans were not working and therefore not paying income taxes, revenues were way down. The U.S. needed to take on more debt.

But in order to do so, Congress would need to vote to raise the debt ceiling. In past years, raising the debt ceiling had hardly been questioned. During George W. Bush's administration, for instance, Congress had voted seven times to raise the debt ceiling. But now a fierce debate began in Congress. Republicans wanted to balance the rise in the debt ceiling with an equal amount of spending cuts. The struggle continued throughout the spring and into the summer of 2011.

Secretary of the Treasury Geithner warned that the debt

ceiling had to be raised by August 2, or a series of disasters would follow: The United States would be unable to pay its debts and would have to default. This would damage the financial reputation of the United States for years to come. Also, the U.S. would have to pay much higher interest rates on its debt, amounting to a tax on all Americans as well as on businesses. Millions of jobs would be lost, and the recession would deepen.

In the end, Congress did vote to raise the debt ceiling, and President Obama was able to sign the bill on August 2, the day of the deadline. But most Americans felt that the long debate over the debt ceiling had been a senseless waste of time. For months, the government had bickered instead of tending to urgent business: putting Americans back to work.

Polls showed that only 13 percent of Americans approved of the job Congress was doing. And only 42 percent approved of the job President Obama was doing. Although Obama's was a better approval rating than Congress's, it was almost the lowest since he had taken the oath of office in January 2009. Many Democrats were disgusted that Obama had tried so hard to compromise with conservative Republicans.

Additionally, some groups that had supported Barack
Obama in 2008, especially Hispanic voters, were disappointed that the president had done little toward reforming
U.S. immigration policy. It was a complicated and difficult
problem. Many Americans blamed immigrants for taking
away U.S. jobs and using U.S. social services. They urged
the government to deport all illegal immigrants, prevent
businesses from hiring them, and increase border security.
Some of the states on the southern border, such as Arizona
and Alabama, were passing new laws of their own to try to
control illegal immigration.

Other Americans argued that the United States was a
nation made up of former immigrants—did we want to
abandon that proud tradition? Others argued that it would
be impossible to remove all of the estimated eleven million
illegal immigrants presently living in the U.S., and very
costly to even try. It would make more sense to set up a
guest worker program and an orderly process for legaliz-
ing immigrants. And immigrants performed vital work
that Americans were not able or willing to do, in spite of
the recession.

During 2011, the economy did not recover as well as
hoped. It grew, but very slowly. Consumers were afraid

to spend money, and businesses were afraid to hire workers. By early 2010, economists estimated that the stimulus package enacted in 2009 had created or saved about two million jobs. But most of the provisions in the stimulus were due to run out by the end of 2011. Hundreds of thousands of workers were about to lose jobs funded by the stimulus money.

State and local governments were still struggling, especially to fund education. State colleges across the country were forced to cut programs and raise tuition fees. Local school boards had to let teachers go, cut programs for students, and put off repairing schools.

The unemployment rate in August 2011 was 9.1 percent, and the extension of unemployment benefits was due to expire at the end of 2011. In contrast, wealthy Americans did not seem to be suffering at all. The U.S. Census Bureau reported that during 2010, the wealthiest 5 percent saw their income rise.

Meanwhile, middle-class families saw their income dwindle. Many ordinary Americans were still angry that the government had saved the big banks from failing. The banks had paid back most of the bailout money, but they had not helped struggling home mortgage-holders or granted loans to small businesses as much as expected. A new protest movement, "Occupy Wall Street," sprang up. Unlike the Tea Party, this new movement blamed their economic hardships on corporate greed and income inequality, rather than on high taxes and government overspending.

On September 8, 2011, President Obama proposed a new stimulus plan to Congress. Called the American Jobs Act, this plan included breaks for small businesses and cuts in payroll taxes. The plan also provided funds to modernize schools, and repair roads and bridges, which would create construction jobs. And aid to state and local governments would put more teachers, police officers, and firefighters back to work. The Jobs Act, Obama explained, would not add to the deficit. Its cost of $447 billion would be paid for through eliminating some tax breaks for wealthier Americans and for corporations.

Taking a newly aggressive tone, the president urged Congress to pass this bill right away. He took a jab at Republicans who might be willing to let the economy stagnate in order to hurt Obama's chances for reelection in November 2012. "The people who sent us here—the people who hired us to work for them—they don't have the luxury of waiting fourteen months."

During the next weeks, President Obama toured the country, asking Americans to demand that Congress pass the Jobs Act. But Republicans, and even some Democrats, voted down the bill, especially criticizing the plan to take away tax breaks for wealthy citizens. The president announced he would come back to Congress with the same proposals, broken down into several smaller bills.

CHAPTER 18

CHANGE TAKES
TIME

MEANWHILE, IN THE FALL OF 2011, THE CAMPAIGN
for the presidential election of 2012 was well under way.
President Obama was assumed to be the Democratic candidate, but his reelection seemed to depend on how voters
felt about the economy.

Although the U.S. economy was slowly improving,
Americans remained worried about jobs. For months, the
number of unemployed Americans had hovered around 9
percent. That is, about 14 million American workers could
not find jobs. Almost half of them had been out of work
for six months or longer. And these figures didn't count
the many workers so discouraged that they had stopped
looking for jobs.

Historians pointed to the example of President Her-
bert Hoover, who was widely blamed for the Great

Depression. In the election of 1932, President Hoover lost to Franklin Roosevelt by a landslide. Likewise, in the election of 1980, President Jimmy Carter had been blamed for the economic slump of that time, and he lost that election to Ronald Reagan by a landslide. And in 1992, during another economic downturn, President George H. W. Bush was defeated by Bill Clinton with the slogan "It's the economy, stupid."

But whether Barack Obama would be reelected or not, he had accomplished some important things.

First of all, he had prevented the country from plunging into a second Great Depression. Not everyone gave him credit for this achievement, however. Americans were still struggling economically, and "Things could have been much worse" does not make a forceful campaign slogan.

President Obama had appointed two women to the Supreme Court: Sonia Sotomayor in 2009 and Elena Kagan in 2010. Before Obama's presidency, only two women had *ever* served on the Supreme Court. Since Supreme Court justices are appointed for life, Justice Sotomayor and Justice Kagan's decisions could continue to affect the law of the nation for many years.

In foreign policy, President Obama had kept his promise

to withdraw combat troops from Iraq, ending the war that he had labeled "dumb" from the beginning. He had focused military efforts on al-Qaeda and succeeded in eliminating several of their leaders, including Osama bin Laden. At the same time, he had set a new tone of cooperation with the rest of the world, and he had relied on diplomacy with other nations to further the interests of the United States.

After other presidents had steadily loosened regulations in the banking industry, Obama put financial reforms in place that were designed to protect consumers.

President Obama cut federal spending in several areas, including ending NASA's space shuttle program and shutting down some expensive weapons programs.

He managed to get Congress to pass a health-care reform bill, after many other presidents had tried and failed. As a result, a million more Americans now had medical coverage, and thirty million more were scheduled to receive coverage in 2014.

However, Barack Obama was not sitting back and admiring his accomplishments. He was more aware than ever that four years was a very short time in which to achieve his goals for the country. If he was not reelected, much of his progress could be rolled back by the next administration. For example, many key parts of the health-care reform act were not scheduled to take effect until 2014.

President Obama saw a great deal of unfinished business. The U.S. budget deficit was almost $15 trillion. It would not be easy to reduce it, with health-care costs growing at an alarming rate. And Obama was determined *not* to reduce the national debt by cutting back investments in important areas, such as education.

Not only did children deserve a good education, Obama believed, but the country needed well-educated citizens. The United States was falling behind other nations economically because it was not preparing enough adults for twenty-first-century jobs.

U.S. immigration policy needed reforming more than ever.

In energy policy, too, President Obama saw much progress to be made. Other countries, such as China, were already investing more in clean-energy industries than the U.S., and the U.S. needed the jobs and prosperity this opportunity offered. Also, the more independent of foreign energy sources the U.S. could become, the better it would be for the country. In his January 2011 State of the Union address, the president foresaw a bright possible future in which the United States could be getting 80 percent of its electricity from clean-energy sources.

Developing clean energy would also work to combat global climate change. If President Obama was elected to a second term, he was determined to focus on this looming threat. Combating climate change would require not only cooperating with other nations, but also convincing the American public that climate change was a grave threat.

Even if Barack Obama was reelected in November 2012, eight years would still not be time enough to accomplish all his goals for the country. "Change is hard," the president told an audience of his supporters in October 2011, "change takes time, but change is possible."

CHAPTER 19

ELECTION 2012

SO FAR, THE AMERICAN PUBLIC APPROVED OF AT least two parts 'of the Patient Protection and Affordable Care Act (ACA). They were happy that children could remain on their parents' health insurance through age twenty-six. And they were even happier that insurance companies could no longer refuse to insure a customer because of "preexisting conditions."

Barack Obama had hoped that as the Affordable Care Act phased in, people would appreciate the program more and more, and resistance would die down. Instead attacks on the ACA continued in several different ways. Incorrect and sometimes absurd rumors spread on the Internet: *Americans without health insurance will be arrested and thrown in jail! The ACA is being funded through a sales tax! ObamaCare*

*includes "death panels" to ration medical care, deciding who will
live and who will die!*

Many Republican politicians, especially if they were
running for office, still vowed to repeal "ObamaCare."
Conservative groups brought lawsuits against the ACA. In
June 2012 the Supreme Court decided to consider whether
the "individual mandate" clause of the ACA was unconstitutional—whether it conflicted with the principles of
the Constitution of the United States. If a majority of the
Supreme Court justices decided that the clause did conflict,
then it would have to be dropped.

The individual mandate clause required most Americans to buy health insurance, or else pay a penalty. The idea
behind this requirement was that younger and healthier
people often assumed that they didn't need health insurance. But if younger and healthier people didn't take part in
the program, the insurance companies would have to charge
higher premiums to the rest of their customers, who were
more likely to need expensive health care. And so many
older, sicker people would not be able to afford insurance,
and they would not receive adequate health care.

Also, even young, healthy people could have accidents

or illness and need expensive medical treatment. If they didn't have insurance, taxpayers would have to pay the bill for them. So the individual mandate was a necessary part of the new health program.

In a close decision, the Supreme Court ruled that this clause was constitutional. However, the Court also decided to allow each state to choose whether they would accept an expansion of their Medicaid program. Medicaid was the program providing health care to Americans too poor to afford it.

At the same time that President Obama's opponents were working to roll back the Affordable Care Act, Michelle Obama's campaign to improve the health of the nation's children was under attack. Back in 2010 Michelle had launched the Let's Move! program to promote more physical activity for children, as well as healthier food in schools and homes. She wanted to educate people about nutrition and health, and to give them the chance to make healthier choices. For instance, in many low-income neighborhoods there were no stores where people could buy fresh fruits and vegetables, and no parks where children could play outside safely.

Let's Move! tied in with one of the key goals of the

ACA, to keep Americans healthy. As it was, only 3 percent of health dollars in the United States were spent on preventing disease, but 75 percent on treating preventable diseases. Promoters of the ACA believed that better preventive care would reduce health care costs. For instance, it costs much less to vaccinate children against measles than to treat the complications from measles: pneumonia, encephalitis, and blindness.

President Obama had supported Let's Move! with a presidential task force to study and plan action on childhood obesity. Obesity, or extreme overweight, had become a major public health crisis, especially among low-income Americans. In 2013 the U.S. Centers for Disease Control and Prevention announced that one in eight preschoolers were obese. Overweight children were likely to become overweight adults, in danger of heart disease, diabetes, and other serious medical problems. These conditions were not only harmful to the patients, but also expensive to treat, further straining the health care system.

Critics of Let's Move! saw it as one more example of big government interfering in Americans' personal lives. But obesity among Americans had even become a problem for the U.S. Department of Defense. Mission: Readiness, a group of retired generals and admirals, spotlighted the problem in their 2010 report "Too Fat to Fight." Department of Defense data showed that 27 percent—more than one-fourth—of U.S. citizens between the ages of seventeen and twenty-four could not qualify for military service because of obesity.

On another important issue, immigration reform, President Obama had tried to promote the DREAM Act. DREAM (Development, Relief, and Education for Alien Minors) aimed to offer a chance at higher education, and even permanent residency in the United States, to a certain group of people living in the country without permission. They had to have been brought to the United States as children, lived here for at least five years, and have no criminal record. This piece of legislation had first been introduced into Congress at the beginning of George W. Bush's presidency, but Congress repeatedly rejected it.

Meanwhile, groups for immigrants' rights were growing impatient with Obama. They accused the president of deporting more immigrants than any president before him. He had certainly increased enforcement at the border with Mexico. On the other hand, in 2011 President Obama had ordered the Immigration and Customs Enforcement

agency (ICE) to concentrate on removing dangerous criminals such as drug dealers, rather than on families. (This was
a common-sense move, since federal agencies did not even
have enough money and manpower to find and deport all
the immigrants who *were* dangerous criminals.)

Obama finally gave up on waiting for Congress to
move on the DREAM Act. In June 2012 he issued an
executive order establishing Deferred Action for Childhood Arrivals (DACA). This program directed U.S. agencies dealing with immigrants, such as ICE, to hold off
on deporting individuals who had been brought to the
United States as children by their illegal immigrant parents and who were now at least fifteen. (Children born in
the territory of the United States automatically become
U.S. citizens by "birthright," even if their parents are in the
country without legal permission.)

The idea behind DACA was similar to that of the
DREAM Act: children who, through no fault of their own,
had grown up in the United States and considered themselves Americans should not be automatically deported.
Through DACA, young illegal immigrants could apply for
two years' reprieve from being deported.

Most Republican candidates for president in 2012

denounced DACA, accusing Obama of encouraging illegal immigration. However, one candidate, Mitt Romney, promised to honor those reprieves if he was elected. And by the end of April 2012, it was clear that Mitt Romney, former governor of Massachusetts, would be the Republican nominee for president.

Romney had two disadvantages: He was a member of the Church of Jesus Christ of Latter-Day Saints, or Mormons, a group that many Americans were unfamiliar or uncomfortable with. Also, he was wealthy, at a time when the richest people were getting richer. In contrast, middle-class people were actually earning less. They were struggling to pay their mortgages and send their children to college.

The year before, the "Occupy Wall Street" protests had made a big point of the fact that the upper 1 percent of Americans earned more than one-fifth of the entire population's income. Also, the "Occupiers" accused the 1 percent— many of them bankers, hedge fund managers, and business leaders—of making the bad decisions that had resulted in the Great Recession of 2007–2009. Unfairly, it was the lower 99 percent of Americans who had suffered most in the recession. In 2009 Congress had raised the U.S. minimum wage to $7.25 per hour, but this was not enough to keep a family out of poverty.

From the beginning of President Obama's campaign for reelection, he emphasized his mission to rebuild the middle class. "This is a make-or-break moment for the middle class and all those who are fighting to get into the middle class," he said. "At stake is whether this will be a country where working people can earn enough to raise a family, build a modest savings, own a home, and secure their retirement."

One issue that received a great deal of attention in the campaign for president was the question of whether same-sex marriage should be legal. In May 2012 Barack Obama made a public statement about his view: "I think same-sex couples should be able to get married."

This was the first time a president had supported same-sex marriage, and Obama's position was sharply different from his Republican opponent's. "I believe marriage is a relationship between a man and a woman," said Mitt Romney. As for Americans in general, they were divided about half and half on the question of same-sex marriage. They were interested in the issue, but it was not nearly as important to them as the economy, and it did not influence the election.

. . .

Meanwhile, in northern Africa, Libya was still in turmoil after the downfall of the dictator Muammar Gaddafi. In September 2012 a group of Islamic militants attacked the U.S. diplomatic compound in Benghazi, Libya. Ambassador Christopher Stevens and three other Americans were killed.

This tragedy became a political advantage for Republicans in the U.S. presidential campaign. Governor Romney and his supporters accused the Obama administration of a weak, confused response to the attack. Also, they blamed the Obama administration for ignoring pleas for better protection from American diplomats in Libya and other countries.

During October the candidates for president debated each other on TV three times. Barack Obama went into the first debate on October 3 with a strong lead in the polls, but he came out of it with his numbers falling. The president's supporters were horrified by his performance. While Governor Romney was energetic and alert, Obama seemed lackluster and detached, as if he wanted to be somewhere else. "Obama wouldn't win a student council election against a chubby nerd," commented a tweet from *Vanity Fair* magazine.

But Obama came back fighting in his following speeches, and toward the end of October he received a boost in public opinion. Only eight days before the election, Hurricane Sandy slammed into the East Coast of the United States, hitting New York and New Jersey especially hard. The storm killed more than one hundred people, swept away pieces of the coastline, and flooded tunnels and subways in New York City. It caused almost as much damage as Hurricane Katrina in 2005, the most expensive hurricane ever in the United States.

Both Romney and Obama dropped their campaign schedules. President Obama flew to New Jersey to see the damage for himself, and to support New Jersey governor Chris Christie. Although Christie was Republican, he praised Obama for his "personal concern and compassion" and for his disaster relief efforts. Pictures of the Republican governor and the Democratic president standing together in the face of disaster were all over the news. To many Americans, weary of gridlock between the parties in Washington politics, this was a welcome sight.

Political scientists believed that Barack Obama would have been reelected in any case, but Hurricane Sandy gave him an extra margin. Americans thought President Obama responded well to the disaster, and they appreciated his sympathy for the victims. On November 6, Election Day,

President Obama won both the popular vote and the majority of electoral votes. The results were not even close.

The campaign for president in 2012 was even more expensive than that of 2008. The Supreme Court had made a ruling in 2010, in the case known as *Citizens United*, which allowed unlimited amounts of money to be given to so-called super PACs. Political action committees, or PACs, are organizations that raise and spend money to elect or defeat a candidate. They can give money directly to a candidate's campaign committee, but they are limited in the amounts they can receive from any one individual, and in the amounts they can donate to any one campaign. Super PACs, on the other hand, are not allowed to contribute directly to political campaigns, but they can act independently to support or oppose a politician.

In 2012 super PACs spent more than a billion dollars trying to influence voters, mainly through TV advertising. However, more of this money had been spent in support of Mitt Romney than Barack Obama. So it seemed that the super PACs did not have the power to swing elections that many people feared.

One reason Mitt Romney had lost, it seemed, was that he appealed mainly to white voters. The nonwhite part of the population, especially Latinos, was steadily growing. According to the U.S. Census Bureau, by the middle of the twenty-first century whites would no longer be the majority. Nonwhite voters tended to see Democrats, more than Republicans, as working for their interests, and they turned out to vote for Barack Obama.

After the election Obama made some changes in his administration. Hillary Clinton was stepping down as secretary of state, and Obama's first choice to replace her would have been Susan Rice, U.S. ambassador to the United Nations. But Republicans criticized Rice severely for her response to the attack on the U.S. diplomats in Benghazi. It was unlikely that the Senate would confirm her, if Obama nominated her. Instead he nominated Senator John Kerry of Massachusetts, who had run for president against George W. Bush in 2004.

An urgent issue for the new secretary of state was the long-running conflict between the State of Israel and the Palestinians within its borders. Immediately after Obama's reelection, war had broken out yet again between Israel and the Palestinian Gaza Strip. The United States was anxious to help solve the Israel-Palestinian problem, because

Israel was a democracy with many ties to Americans, and a reliable ally of the United States in the Middle East.

Before Barack Obama took the oath of office for his second term, a tragedy marred his political victory. This violence took place not in the war-torn Middle East, but in Newtown, Connecticut. On December 14, 2012, a mentally unstable youth entered an elementary school and shot twenty children and six adults, as well as himself. In January, President Obama proposed several measures to solve the problem of gun violence. Among these measures, he urged Congress to pass two gun control laws: a law requiring that anyone buying a gun should have a background check, to make sure they did not have a record of mental illness or crimes; and a law banning "military-style assault weapons," which were not needed for either hunting or self-defense.

Most Americans were in favor of background checks and assault weapons bans. Gabrielle Giffords, a former congresswoman from Arizona, spoke out for gun control. She herself had been shot in the head in 2011, when a gunman killed six people and wounded fourteen others in Tucson. But the influence of the National Rifle Association, which interpreted the Second Amendment of the

Constitution as guaranteeing the right of American citizens to own and use guns with few restrictions, was too strong. The proposed gun control laws were defeated in Congress.

President Obama gave his second inaugural address on January 21, 2013, which was also Martin Luther King Jr. Day. The president emphasized what he saw as the biggest challenges of his second term: reducing poverty and injustice in the United States and combating global climate change. "We will respond to the threat of climate change, knowing that the failure to do so would betray our children and future generations."

Although billions of dollars had been spent on the 2012 election campaigns, the political situation in the United States had not really changed. Barack Obama was still president. Republicans still controlled the House of Representatives, and Democrats still controlled the Senate.

Most important, the conservative Republicans and the liberal Democrats seemed as bitterly opposed as before. They saw each other as not just opponents, but enemies. That made it difficult for them to work together to solve the problems facing the whole country.

CHAPTER 20

A HAILSTORM
OF TROUBLES

LYNDON JOHNSON, WHO WAS PRESIDENT DURING the troubled Vietnam War years, was from Texas, where hailstones as large as baseballs could fall. Johnson once advised President Richard Nixon (who was forced to resign from the office in 1974), "The presidency is like being a jackass in a hailstorm. You've got to just stand there and take it." The first year of Barack Obama's second term was riddled with a hailstorm of troubles.

On April 15, 2013, another act of violence shocked the nation. Bombs exploding in the crowds at the yearly Boston Marathon race killed three people and injured hundreds more. Shortly afterward, President Obama addressed the nation, assuring Americans that the bombers would be identified, would be caught, and would "feel the full weight of justice." He ordered the flags on the White House and on federal buildings throughout the country to be lowered to half-mast as a mark of respect for the victims. A few days later the president flew to Boston to speak at an interfaith service honoring the victims of the bombing.

At first it was feared that this attack was another plot by a terrorist group such as al-Qaeda. But it turned out that the bombs were set off near the Boston Marathon finish line by two brothers originally from Chechnya, a Russian republic that was once part of the Soviet Union. Although the young men were influenced by Islamic extremists, they were acting by themselves. In the manhunt following the bombing, the older brother was killed, but the younger brother was captured. In 2015 he was tried and convicted.

A president's first duty, as leader of the United States of America and commander in chief of its armed forces, is to keep the country safe from attacks. One of the president's tools for discovering and foiling such attacks is the National Security Agency (NSA). This agency collects enormous amounts of information from all over the world and sifts out data that seem to reveal threats to the United States. In 2009 information gathered by the NSA helped to thwart a plot to bomb the New York City subway.

But in June 2013, a scandal involving the NSA broke,

embarrassing the Obama administration and alarming U.S. citizens as well as foreign countries. Edward Snowden, a former NSA contractor, made public a large number of top secret files. The files showed that the NSA had been collecting data, including phone call and e-mail records, not just on suspected spies or terrorists, but also on millions of ordinary Americans. The telephone company Verizon, for instance, had handed over phone call records to the NSA without the knowledge or consent of its customers. This surveillance had begun during George W. Bush's presidency, but it had continued after Barack Obama became president.

Immediately after Snowden's revelation, President Obama went before the cameras to assure the country that NSA's data collection helped to prevent terrorist attacks. The NSA looked at the phone numbers called, and the length of the calls, he explained. But it did not invade Americans' privacy by listening to what was said in the conversations.

Many Americans were not reassured, especially young Americans. President Obama's approval rating dropped from 53 percent in May to 45 percent in June, according to a CNN/ORC opinion poll. Several protest groups, such as Restore the Fourth, sprang up. The Fourth Amendment to the Constitution, part of the Bill of Rights, forbids "unreasonable searches" by the government. The protesters saw the NSA's massive data collection as clearly unreasonable and unnecessary.

The secret files leaked by Snowden also revealed that the NSA had spied on allies and partners, as well as on countries hostile to the United States. Angela Merkel, chancellor of Germany, was furious to learn that the NSA had tapped her personal cell phone. "Spying between friends, that's just not done," she commented at a press conference.

In a strained private conversation with President Obama, Merkel told him that the NSA obviously couldn't be trusted with secret information, or how had it allowed Edward Snowden to reveal it? President Obama assured Chancellor Merkel that the United States would not spy on her cell phone again. But the incident was a major diplomatic embarrassment.

President Obama would rather have concentrated on the problem of income inequality in the United States. As he had explained in his State of the Union speech in February 2013, he thought that education was the key to allowing Americans to move into the middle class. High-quality preschool for everyone was especially important, to make sure that even children from poor families were prepared for formal education and the opportunities it offered.

As it was, children from low-income homes often entered kindergarten without the necessary experience to succeed in school. They were behind the other children from the beginning, and they struggled year after year. Many finally dropped out without graduating from high school.

In the same State of the Union speech, President Obama had called upon Congress to raise the minimum wage, which was not enough to support a family above the poverty level. But Congress had not taken action. Republicans argued that forcing a raise in the minimum wage would hurt businesses and cause workers to lose jobs.

At the end of August 2013, fast-food workers in sixty cities across the United States walked off their jobs. They were protesting their wages, the federal minimum of $7.25 per hour. Most fast-food workers were not teenagers earning pocket money, but adults trying to feed their families and pay the rent.

The rising cost of medical care added to the plight of many low-income workers. They could not afford medical insurance, and depending on which state they lived in, they were not necessarily covered by Medicaid. During

222

2013, 42 million people in the United States had no health insurance. President Obama and his team intended that the Affordable Care Act, by making health care insurance available to almost all Americans, would lighten the burden of income inequality.

In October the Centers for Medicare and Medicaid Services, an agency of the U.S. Department of Health and Human Services, launched HealthCare.gov. This website was supposed to make it easy for Americans to compare the prices of different health insurance policies. The idea was also that Americans could find out if they qualified for a subsidy, which would make up the difference between what they could afford to pay and the cost of a basic health insurance policy. And people eligible for Medicaid could sign up for that program.

Unfortunately, the private companies hired by the Department of Health and Human Services badly bungled the launch of HealthCare.gov. The website had many technical problems. At first hardly anyone trying to enroll in a health insurance plan was successful. There were long waits to log on to the site, and more long waits after that.

Trying to enroll was so frustrating that *Consumer Reports*, a popular magazine that reviews and rates goods and services for customers, advised insurance shoppers to stay away from the site for a month. *Consumer Reports* did not oppose the Affordable Care Act, but they estimated it would be at least a month before the problems could be ironed out. President Obama told a press conference in the Rose Garden, "No one's madder than me about the website not working as well as it should."

Luckily for the Obama administration, at the same time as the botched rollout of HealthCare.gov, Congress distracted the country with a government shutdown. During the first sixteen days in October, they failed to agree on a budget to run the government for the year 2014. The Republican-majority House voted to discontinue funding "ObamaCare," as they called the Affordable Care Act. But the Democratic-majority Senate voted the funds for ACA back in.

During this deadlock, the federal government ran out of money and closed for two weeks. Many government agencies were affected. The national parks, including monuments in Washington, DC, were closed. Most Americans blamed Congress, rather than President Obama, for the shutdown.

In spite of this distraction, it seemed as if the mismanaged rollout of HealthCare.gov might cause the ACA to fail. Many people trying to use the website to sign up got discouraged.

Many others, even if they were eligible for subsidies, didn't try. The government's goal was to sign up 500,000 more uninsured Americans during October 2013 alone. But by the end of November, only 365,000 had managed to sign up.

Outside the United States, Obama was on course to completely withdraw U.S. troops from Afghanistan by the end of 2014. The war in Afghanistan had lasted ten years, and more than two thousand U.S. soldiers had died. It seemed that the goal of weakening al-Qaeda, the Islamic militants who had attacked the United States on September 11, 2001, had been achieved. The United States had also removed from power the Taliban, the Islamic fundamentalists who gave al-Qaeda safe haven. Sadly, it seemed likely that when the U.S. troops and their allies left Afghanistan, the Taliban would take over again.

But many other regions of the world demanded President Obama's attention, especially the troubled Middle East. Like many other U.S. presidents before him, he hoped to help make peace between Israel and the Palestinians. He believed that the only realistic solution was for Israel to allow Palestine to become a separate nation.

During 2013, Secretary of State John Kerry worked

hard to get the two sides to stop fighting and start talking. After several months of diplomacy, Kerry managed to persuade the Palestinians and Israelis to agree to a series of talks, with the goal of reaching a solution by April 2014. But instead the talks broke down at that time. Obama doubted that Israeli prime minister Benjamin Netanyahu was serious about working toward a two-state solution.

Also in the Middle East, Iran had been an avowed enemy of the United States ever since the Iranian Revolution in 1979. Iran did not possess nuclear weapons, but it was conducting research that could lead to such weapons. And Israel feared that it would be the first target of any nuclear weapons that Iran developed. In January 2014 President Obama was able to announce that Iran was cutting back on its nuclear program and had promised to allow inspection of its nuclear facilities. In return, the United States and its allies would lift some of the economic sanctions that were hurting Iran's economy.

From Syria, there was nothing but bad news. The civil war against President Bashar al-Assad, which had broken out in 2011, continued to rage. By August 2013, millions of Syrians had fled to neighboring countries. The United States contributed millions of dollars' worth of relief goods, such as food and medical supplies, to the United Nations' humanitarian response for the refugees.

Syria was a difficult and complicated problem. Some in Congress, as well as Secretary of State Kerry, thought that the United States should help the rebels overthrow Assad. He was a brutal dictator who had used poison gas against his own citizens, most of them civilians. But President Obama did not want to get involved in yet another Middle Eastern war. The United States had only recently withdrawn from Iraq, and American soldiers were still engaged in Afghanistan.

Furthermore, Obama and many of his advisers were uncertain how much the United States could help the Syrian rebels by intervening. Also, some of the groups fighting Assad's regime were Islamic extremists, enemies of the United States, who intended to establish their own dictatorship in Syria. However, the United States did provide small arms and ammunition to support the moderate rebel groups. In the United Nations, the Security Council attempted to place economic sanctions on Syria, but Russia and China both vetoed the proposal.

Russia was increasingly worrisome to the Obama administration in several ways. Under President Vladimir Putin, the country was moving further away from democratic rule. Former president George W. Bush had tried, without much success, to influence Putin by becoming friends with him.

Barack Obama, during his first term, had tried to improve relations with Russia by working with the new Russian president, Dmitry Medvedev. But in 2012 Putin took over the presidency of Russia again. He clamped down on political opposition within Russia, and he worked to expand Russia's influence over Eastern Europe and Asia and to pull away from the West.

As if to demonstrate that Russia didn't need the friendship of the United States, Vladimir Putin gave asylum to Edward Snowden, the NSA employee who had leaked secret files. In March 2014 Putin sent Russian troops into southeastern Ukraine. A few weeks later he boldly annexed the Crimean peninsula, a section of Ukraine, to Russia.

Since the end of the Cold War with the Soviet Union in 1991, Americans had not worried much about Russia. But when Russia took over the Crimea, they suddenly saw Russia as a threat to the United States again.

Now and then, Barack Obama took time out from the hailstorm of troubles pelting his presidency to play golf. It was a way for him to "relax and clear my head," he said. The media ran pictures of the president on the golf course, and many Republicans criticized him. However, Obama got a kind word from former president George W. Bush, who knew how stressful the job was. "I think he ought to play golf," said Bush. "To be able to get outside and play golf with some of your pals is important for the president."

In the summer of 2013, the president announced a piece of news that everyone could love. The Obamas were adopting a new dog, Sunny, a Portuguese water dog, like Bo. The White House released pictures of the First Family walking their new pet outside, and of the new dog romping with the First Dog on the White House lawn. The president explained that Bo had needed a frisky young companion to play with. The Obamas didn't say so, but Sunny could also have been a model for Michelle's Let's Move! campaign.

"If Congress won't act soon to protect future generations, I will," President Obama had promised in his 2013 State of the Union speech. Obama could not persuade Congress to pass legislation to reduce greenhouse gas emissions, but he did order the Environmental Protection Agency (EPA) to apply a series of new regulations, summarized in the

Climate Action Plan of 2013. Through the EPA, Obama required stricter emission standards for cars, light trucks, and heavy trucks. He also set stricter pollution standards for coal-fired plants.

Under the Clean Air Act, first passed in 1970, the EPA was supposed to regulate emissions harmful to human beings. However, during George W. Bush's presidency, the EPA had not enforced the law energetically. Most Americans supported President Obama's new regulations. Even Americans who were skeptical about climate change still favored restraints on pollution, for the sake of clean air.

At the end of 2013, President Obama made a special trip to South Africa for a memorial service. His hero Nelson Mandela, the first black president of South Africa, had died at the age of ninety-five. Mandela had been revered around the world as a peacemaker, and Obama had hoped to follow his example by making peace between the battling factions in the United States. But with elections for Congress coming up in 2014, that hope seemed fainter than ever.

CHAPTER 21

JUST GET STUFF DONE

DURING 2014, AMERICANS SEEMED SUNK IN A MOST un–American mood: anxious and pessimistic about the future. True, the U.S. economy slowly continued to improve. The unemployment rate dropped below 6 per-cent, the lowest since 2008. However, most Americans did not see the economic improvement that mattered most to them—an increase in their paychecks. President Obama was well aware of this income inequality problem, which he called "the defining challenge of our time."

As the year went on, some dramatic events caused Americans more uncertainty and worry. In West Africa, an outbreak of the deadly Ebola virus grew into an epi-demic. Ebola was a truly terrifying disease, killing most of its victims unless they were diagnosed early and treated with the best medical care. By August the World Health

Organization (WHO) declared the epidemic an international health emergency. And in October, Thomas Duncan, a Liberian traveling from West Africa to the United States, died of Ebola in a Dallas hospital.

Even though only one Ebola patient had died in America, the media gave the case a great deal of attention, and many people got the impression that Ebola was a serious threat in the United States. Panic spread, and the Republican politicians running for senator, congressman, or governor criticized the Obama administration's response to the disease. Some candidates tried to link the public's fear of Ebola with immigration problems, suggesting that Democratic policies would allow immigrants infected with Ebola to cause an epidemic in the United States. (Actually, no cases of Ebola had been reported in Central America, or in any part of Latin America.)

But many Americans were already worried about immigration. A tidal wave of young people, unaccompanied by their parents, was pouring over the Mexican border. Nearly 60,000 children under the age of seventeen had entered the United States illegally within the last year. They came from Central America, fleeing for their lives from some of the most violent countries in the world. It seemed that they and their parents had the mistaken idea that once they crossed the U.S. border, they would be allowed to stay.

In the summer of 2014, the news was full of pictures of young immigrants traveling north through Mexico by clinging to the tops of trains. On the U.S. side of the border, they slept side by side on the floors of emergency shelters. President Obama assured Americans that the undocumented youngsters would be sent back to their countries, but meanwhile he asked Congress for $3.7 billion to house and feed them. The Department of Homeland Security was overwhelmed with all the new cases awaiting the immigration court process leading to asylum or deportation.

In some parts of the United States, residents were angry when immigrants were placed in their communities. Protesters with signs like RETURN TO SENDER greeted buses bringing young immigrants. By law, even undocumented children had to attend school where they lived, and school districts were resentful of the extra burden. Many school districts asked the federal government for money to pay for interpreters, extra teachers, and extra school buildings.

Republicans blamed President Obama for the unaccompanied alien children (UAC) crisis. They charged that his DACA action, allowing young undocumented

233

immigrants who had grown up in the United States to remain, had given illegal immigrants false hope. The Obama administration likewise blamed Republicans in the House of Representatives for the crisis. They had failed to vote on, or even debate, the immigration reform bill already approved by the Senate last year.

Outside the United States, in the Middle East, loomed another cause for Americans to worry about the future: the extremist Islamic group calling itself the Islamic State of Iraq and Syria (ISIS). In June 2014, ISIS proclaimed a worldwide caliphate, or authority, over all the one and a half billion Muslims worldwide. ISIS launched an all-out attack on northern Iraq, and they quickly seized control of several key cities.

President Obama decided to help defend Iraq with air strikes against ISIS targets, and most members of Congress, Republicans as well as Democrats, agreed. The U.S. public also supported the air strikes, although they were uneasy that the United States might get drawn into another war in Iraq and Syria.

Voters in the United States were usually much more concerned with the state of the U.S. economy than about issues in the outside world. But in August, when ISIS executed an American journalist in a grisly manner, this foreign threat jumped into the U.S. headlines. Several other such executions, of people from other countries as well as Americans, followed. As the United States, as well as European and Arab allies, continued air strikes against in Iraq and Syria, ISIS threatened to retaliate with attacks on the United States and its allies.

In Eastern Europe, Russia had seized the Crimea and was still threatening eastern Ukraine. Some members of Congress urged President Obama to support Ukraine with military force. If Obama acted tougher, they said, Putin would not dare to be so aggressive.

Obama demanded that Russia withdraw its troops from eastern Ukraine, but he thought it would be a big mistake to risk a war with Russia. The United States did join with other nations to punish Russia with economic sanctions. By the end of the year, the price of oil, which was Russia's major export, had dropped sharply. The Russian economy was in serious trouble.

Back home, Americans were disturbed to learn of security failures in the Secret Service, which guards the safety of the president. Every president in recent times, including Barack Obama, had been threatened with assassination.

Four times in U.S. history, beginning with Abraham Lincoln in 1865 and ending with John F. Kennedy in 1963, the assassins had succeeded. Presidents accepted this danger as part of their job, assuming that the Secret Service was always striving to protect them more effectively.

In September 2014 a man armed with a knife jumped the fence at the White House and ran across the North Lawn. According to security protocol, he should have been stopped by White House guards, the attack dog, or the guard assigned to the front door. Instead the intruder entered the unlocked front door and ran through the mansion.

A guard finally tackled the intruder in the East Room. Later, Julia Pierson, the director of the Secret Service, was forced to resign for allowing such lax security in this and other instances, and for not fully informing the president.

In the effort to apply the Affordable Care Act, the Obama administration had learned from its mistakes in 2013. The HealthCare.gov website was greatly improved, and millions more Americans bought health insurance in 2014. The newly insured people no longer had to choose between going bankrupt trying to pay medical bills or simply doing without health care. Additional millions more were expected to sign up in 2015.

However, an important part of the Affordable Care Act was expanding Medicaid, the program offering health care to low-income Americans. Although Medicaid was a national program, it was administered by the states. The Supreme Court had ruled that each state had the right to accept or reject the ACA expansion of Medicaid, along with the money to pay for it. So far, twenty-one states had refused to expand their Medicaid programs. In these states, not nearly as many low-income residents became insured.

Meanwhile, many Democratic senators were running for reelection in 2014. President Barack Obama was still unpopular with voters, with an approval rating around 42 percent. Republican challengers accused the Obama administration of "killing jobs" by enforcing environmental regulations—requiring businesses to spend more money to avoid polluting, for instance, and consequently having less money to pay their workers. Or "killing jobs" by allowing illegal immigrants, who might work for less and therefore take jobs from U.S. citizens, into the country.

Republicans campaigned by tying each Democratic

candidate to Obama, while the Democrats tried to avoid even mentioning the president. Almost none of them wanted Obama to campaign with them. The Democratic candidate for U.S. senator in Kentucky refused to say whether she had ever voted for Barack Obama.

Much the same thing had happened to President George W. Bush in 2006, when his approval rating was even lower (38 percent). But Barack Obama thought it was a mistake for Democratic candidates to pretend they had no connection to him. Instead he thought they should remind voters of how much his administration had accomplished: the economic recovery, the benefits of the Affordable Care Act, and the winding-down of the wars in Iraq and Afghanistan.

One new factor in the elections of 2014 was a change to the Voting Rights Act of 1965. This law had ensured that the states could not pass laws that restricted voting, as many Southern states had done after the Civil War to keep African-Americans from the polls. But in June 2013 the Supreme Court made a ruling that weakened the Voting Rights Act. The court struck down Section 4(b) of the act.

Section 4(b) gave the formula by which Congress determined which states and local governments had discriminated against African-American voters, or other groups of voters, in the past. Such state and local governments, according to the Voting Rights Act, must get approval from the attorney general of the United States for any changes in voting laws. With Section 4(b) gone, several conservative states adopted new laws about election procedures.

Some of the new laws required voters to present a photo ID, such as a driver's license, to prove that they were U.S. citizens. Other laws cut back on weekend hours at the polls and early voting. These changes made it more difficult for many low-income citizens, as well as the handicapped and elderly, to cast their ballots. They did not have the time, or the physical ability, to wait in long lines to vote. Many of them did not drive, and getting a photo ID just for voting was an extra hurdle.

Since people in these groups tended to vote Democratic, Democrats accused Republicans of trying to reduce support for the Democratic candidates. And it was true that many of the young, black, or Latino voters who had reelected Obama in 2012 did not show up at the polls. In some cases, they could have swung the election results in favor of the Democratic candidates.

It was hard to say how much the new voting laws had to do with it, but the outcome of Election Day 2014 was clear. Republicans gained nine seats in the Senate, to win the majority. In the House of Representatives, they picked up thirteen seats. Republicans had not been so dominant in Congress since 1929. Throughout the country, Republicans rejoiced. They proclaimed that President Obama would be a "lame duck," unable to accomplish any of his goals for the rest of his second term.

Republicans were sure that the voters had signaled approval of their conservative agenda. But Obama thought the American public wanted the politicians to stop squabbling and get out of Washington gridlock, in which no laws were passed because Republicans and Democrats could not work together. He saw the election as the message "Just get stuff done."

In a press conference the day after the election, Obama pointed out issues on which both Democrats and Republicans might agree. For instance, around the country, bridges and roadways were dangerously in need of repair. If Congress decided to act on this problem, the government could both repair the crumbling infrastructure and, at the same time, create many thousands of well-paying jobs.

The president also pointed out a positive note in the

election results: although Congress had failed to pass a federal minimum wage increase this year, five states had just voted to increase their minimum wage. This was a hopeful step toward Obama's goal of narrowing the income gap between the 99 percent and the top 1 percent.

As for Republican threats to roll back the Affordable Care Act, or "ObamaCare," President Obama was calmly determined to veto any such bills from Congress. And if Congress did not pass an immigration reform bill before the end of 2014, he would go ahead with executive actions. "What we can't do is just keep on waiting. There is a cost to waiting."

In mid-November President Obama left for China, Myanmar, and Australia. The public purpose of the trip was to attend meetings on increasing trade between the United States and Asian nations. However, in Beijing, Barack Obama and Chinese president Xi Jinping had a surprise announcement for the world.

The two leaders had agreed on a landmark plan to combat climate change. Each nation promised to make deep cuts in the emission of greenhouse gases. Since the United States and China were the two biggest carbon dioxide polluters in the world, their actions could make an important difference.

And as two of the most powerful nations in the world, they could lead other countries to follow their example. This agreement set a hopeful tone for the United Nations Climate Change meetings to come in 2015.

With this bold action, Obama also seemed to be sending a message back home: Look, you may think I'm a lame duck, but I can still make big things happen. I'm still the president of the United States of America.

Back in Washington, President Obama continued to take the measures he thought were best for the country, whether Republicans went along or not. As he explained, "The future rewards those who press on. I don't have time to feel sorry for myself. I don't have time to complain. I'm going to press on."

Obama "pressed on" through executive actions, giving orders that did not need to be approved by Congress. In the past, different presidents had issued hundreds of such orders. Among the most important, President Theodore Roosevelt created many national parks, national forests, national monuments, and wildlife refuges by executive order. President Harry Truman accomplished the racial integration of the U.S. military by executive order.

On November 20, 2014, President Obama announced his executive action on immigration: a halt to deportation proceedings against five million undocumented immigrants who had not committed a crime, other than illegal entry. They could also apply for work permits.

Republicans were outraged. "We will not stand idle as the president undermines the rule of law in our country," said John A. Boehner, Speaker of the House of Representatives. But as President Obama noted, Congress was free to overrule him. If the Republicans and Democrats in the Senate and House of Representatives could work together and pass a law on immigration reform, that would replace the president's executive order.

In December, the president acted on his belief that early childhood education was the key to reducing income inequality. He announced that more than $1 billion of federal money would be available for early childhood education programs. Many states had already been awarded grants.

That same month Obama made a bold move to restore full relations with Cuba, the island nation only ninety miles from the tip of Florida. For the first time since 1961, the United States would have an embassy in Havana, and trade and travel restrictions would be loosened. Many Republicans in

Congress vowed not to cooperate. However, some Republicans agreed with the president that the United States' closed-door policy had only helped to keep the repressive Castro regime in power.

When Barack Obama was elected as the first African-American president in 2008, many of his supporters hoped that a new era of racial harmony had begun in the United States. Instead most black Americans continued to feel that they were not treated fairly, especially by the police. This issue came to a head at the end of 2014 with two widely publicized cases, one in Ferguson, Missouri, and the other in Staten Island, New York.

In each case, it was discovered that an unarmed black man had been killed by a police officer. In each case, the police officer was not brought to trial. All around the country, thousands of demonstrators joined in protesting the decisions.

President Obama responded, "When anybody in this country is not being treated equally under the law, that's a problem, and it's my job as president to help solve it." He announced that the government would provide $75 million to police forces nationwide for body cameras. When police officers wore body cameras, there were not so many disagreements about the facts of an incident. Also, police officers with cameras tended to be more careful about using force.

The U.S. Department of Justice launched an investigation of the Ferguson Police Department records between 2012 and 2014. In March 2015 they reported that the Ferguson police had routinely acted with racial bias toward African-American citizens. The police had violated the Constitution, as well as federal law.

March 2015 also marked the fiftieth anniversary of the civil rights protest march from Selma, Alabama, to the state capital, Montgomery. On March 7, 1965, a peaceful group demonstrating for voting rights had been beaten and tear-gassed by police officers. The incident shocked Americans, raising their awareness of racial injustice, and spurred Congress to pass the Voting Rights Act of 1965.

On March 7, 2015, Barack Obama spoke to thousands of people assembled in Selma to commemorate the events of 1965. Two other speakers were the civil rights pioneer John Lewis, who had suffered a fractured skull during the historic march, and the current governor of Alabama, Robert Bentley. The audience included former president George W. Bush and many Republican, as well as Democratic, members of Congress.

President Obama noted that the nation had made great progress in race relations since 1965, but also that there was more work to be done. He spoke passionately of what makes America special among the nations of the world. To Obama, America meant "We, the people," as the Constitution of the United States begins.

"We," Obama repeated over and over, emphasizing that all Americans are equally part of this exceptional country. *We*, striving and risking and sacrificing in many different ways. "We respect the past, but we don't pine for the past. We don't fear the future; we grab for it."

To the audience in Selma and to all the Americans listening, hoping for inspiration, Barack Obama gave his definition of true patriotism: "the belief that America is not yet finished, that we are strong enough to be self-critical, that each successive generation can look upon our imperfections and decide that it is in our power to remake this nation to more closely align with our highest ideals."

TIME LINE

August 4, 1961: Barack Hussein Obama is born in Honolulu, Hawaii.

1967: BHO moves to Indonesia to live with his mother and stepfather.

1970: Half sister, Maya, is born in Indonesia.

1971: BHO returns to Honolulu, Hawaii, to live with his grandparents.

1979: BHO goes to Occidental College in Los Angeles, California.

1981: BHO makes his first public speech. He urges that Occidental support the abolishment of apartheid in South Africa.

1983: BHO graduates from Columbia University in New York City (he transferred there in his junior year).

1988: BHO attends Harvard Law School in Boston, Massachusetts.

1990: BHO becomes the first black president of the *Harvard Law Review*.

1991: BHO graduates from Harvard Law School.

1992: BHO marries Michelle Robinson in Chicago, Illinois.

1993: BHO joins Davis, Miner, Barnhill & Galland, a Chicago law firm that specializes in civil rights legislation.

TIME LINE

1995: *Dreams from My Father*, BHO's first memoir, goes on sale.

1996: BHO is elected Illinois state senator.

1998: Daughter Malia Ann is born.

1999: BHO runs for Congress but loses to Republican candidate Bobby Rush.

2001: Second daughter, Sasha, is born.

2002: BHO is reelected to the Illinois State Senate.

July 2004: BHO gives the keynote speech at the Democratic National Convention in Boston and is elected to the United States Senate later in the year.

2007: BHO begins campaigning for the presidency of the United States.

August 2008: BHO announces Senator Joseph Robinette "Joe" Biden Jr., as his running mate.

November 4, 2008: BHO becomes the forty-fourth president of the United States.

May 2009: BHO nominates Sonia Sotomayor to the Supreme Court.

October 9, 2009: BHO is awarded the Nobel Peace Prize.

February 2010: Michelle Obama launches the Let's Move! campaign.

March 23, 2010: BHO signs the Patient Protection and Affordable Care Act.

July 21, 2010: BHO signs the bill that will regulate banks in the future.

September 17, 2011: Occupy Wall Street protests begin in New York City.

TIME LINE

May 2, 2011: BHO announces the death of Osama bin Laden, the man responsible for the attacks on September 11, 2001.

November 6, 2012: BHO and Vice President Joe Biden are reelected for a second term.

May 2012: BHO announces support for the legalization of same-sex marriage.

June 2012: BHO issues an executive order establishing Deferred Action for Childhood Arrivals (DACA).

September 2012: A group of Islamic militants attacks the U.S. diplomatic compound in Benghazi, Libya.

November 2013: BHO orders the Environmental Protection Agency (EPA) to apply a series of new regulations, summarized in the Climate Action Plan of 2013.

August 2014: The World Health Organization (WHO) declares the Ebola epidemic an international health emergency.

November 2014: BHO and Chinese president Xi Jinping announce agreement on a landmark plan to combat climate change.

November 20, 2014: BHO announces his executive action on immigration: a halt to deportation proceedings against five million undocumented immigrants who have not committed a crime.

December 2014: BHO announces that more than $1 billion of federal money will be available for early childhood education programs.

March 7, 2015: BHO speaks to thousands of people assembled in Selma, Alabama, to commemorate the fiftieth anniversary of the Selma to Montgomery march of 1965, part of the voting rights movement.

SOURCES

BOOKS

Alter, Jonathan. *The Promise: President Obama, Year One.* New York: Simon & Schuster, 2010.

Balz, Dan. *Collision 2012: Obama vs. Romney and the Future of Elections in America.* New York: Viking (Penguin Group), 2013.

Mendell, David. *Obama: From Promise to Power.* New York: HarperCollins, 2007.

Obama, Barack. *The Audacity of Hope: Thoughts on Reclaiming the American Dream.* New York: Three Rivers Press, 2007.

———. *Dreams from My Father: A Story of Race and Inheritance.* New York: Times Books, 1995.

Remnick, David. *The Bridge: The Life and Rise of Barack Obama.* New York: Knopf, 2010.

MAGAZINES AND NEWSPAPERS

Anderton, Trish. "Obama's Jakarta Trail." *The Jakarta Post,* July 22, 2008.

Argetsinger, Amy, and Roxanne Roberts. "The Obama Family's Multicultural Weapons." *The Washington Post,* January 22, 2008.

Associated Press. "Obama Views Children's Health Bill As Step One." February 5, 2009.

Baker, Peter. "Obama offers liberal vision: We must act." *The New York Times,* January 21, 2013.

———. "Nation's confidence ebbs at a steady drip." *The New York Times,* October 21, 2014.

Baker, Peter, and Fausset, Richard. "Work of Selma, Obama says, is 'not over yet.'" *The New York Times,* March 7, 2015.

SOURCES

Balz, Dan, and Clement, Scott. "Divide over police is also partisan." *The Washington Post*, December 28, 2014.

Barker, Kim. "History of Schooling Distorted." *Chicago Tribune*, March 25, 2007.

Baxter, Sarah. "White House Hopeful's 'Lost' Sister Lives in Britain." *London Times*, November 5, 2006.

Belasco, Amy. "The Cost of Iraq, Afghanistan and Other Global War on Terror Operations Since 9/11." Congressional Research Service, March 29, 2011.

Broder, John M. "Obama to Open Offshore Areas to Oil Drilling for First Time." *The New York Times*, March 31, 2010.

Burnett, Sara. "Coloradan Zazi's coded e-mail started agency's plan to stop N.Y. subway attack." *The Denver Post*, October 2, 2011.

Calmes, Jackie, and Cooper, Michael. "New Consensus Sees Stimulus Package as Worthy Step." *The New York Times*, November 20, 2009.

Collins, Lauren. "The Other Obama." *The New Yorker*, March 10, 2008.

Committee on Armed Services, United States Senate. "Inquiries into the Treatment of Detainees in U.S. Custody." November 20, 2008.

The Commonwealth Fund, *2008 Annual Report*.

Davis, Julie Hirschfield, and Weisman, Jonathan. "Bipartisan support, with caveats, for Obama on Iraq airstrikes." *The New York Times*, August 8, 2014.

Emanuel, Ezekiel J. "How Much Does Health Cost?" *The New York Times*, October 30, 2011.

Fornek, Scott. "Auma Obama: 'Her Restlessness, Her Independence.'" *Chicago Sun-Times*, September 9, 2007.

——. "Madelyn Payne Dunham: 'A Trailblazer.'" *Chicago Sun-Times*, September 9, 2007.

Gold, Matea, and Mason, Melanie. "Effect of 'super pacs' proved to be less than expected." *Los Angeles Times*, November 8, 2012.

SOURCES

Goodnough, Abby. "Poll on Health Care Law Shows Increased Support." *The New York Times*, March 19, 2015.

Grier, Peter. "Michelle Obama says 'Let's Move' on obesity in American kids." *The Christian Science Monitor*, February 9, 2010.

Hampson, Rick. "Afghanistan: America's Longest War." *USA Today*, May 28, 2010.

Harwood, John. "A Go-It-Alone Push Fits the Times." *The New York Times*, December 8, 2014.

Hertsgaard, Mark. "Promises, promises," *Harper's*, July 2014, pp. 28–35.

Jones, Tim. "Barack Obama: Mother Not Just a Girl from Kansas." *Chicago Tribune*, March 27, 2007.

Kantor, Jodi. "In 2008 Race, Little Ones Go on the Trail With Daddy." *The New York Times*, August 26, 2007.

Kelemen, Michele. "U.N. Envoy Nominee Rice Known as Tough, Smart." All Things Considered (National Public Radio), December 1, 2008.

Kiefer, Francine. "Is Obama 'Deporter in Chief'? A rundown of the numbers." *The Christian Science Monitor*, April 5, 2014.

Luft, Oliver. "Web Traffic Soars for Obama Inauguration." *The Guardian*, January 22, 2009.

Memoli, Michael L. "Mitch McConnell's Remarks on 2012 Draw White House Ire." *Los Angeles Times*, October 27, 2010.

Merida, Kevin. "The Ghost of a Father." *The Washington Post*, December 14, 2007.

———. "Oxy Remembers 'Barry' Obama '83." *Occidental College Bulletin*, January 29, 2007.

Obama, Barack. "Oval Office Address on Iraq." Transcript, *The Washington Post*, August 31, 2010.

SOURCES

Pippenger, Nathan. *Commonweal*, September 9, 2011. "Commander-in-Chief of Nuance."

Reuters. "U.S. CBO Estimates 2.4 Trillion Long-Term War Costs." October 24, 2007.

Reyes, B. J. "Punahou Left Lasting Impression on Obama." *Honolulu Star-Bulletin*, February 8, 2007.

Ripley, Amanda. "The Story of Barack Obama's Mother." *Time*, April 9, 2008.

Risen, James, and Poitras, Laura. "N.S.A. gathers data on social connections of U.S. citizens." *The New York Times*, September 28, 2013.

Robertson, Campbell, and Krauss, Clifford. "Gulf Spill Is the Largest of Its Kind, Scientists Say." *The New York Times*, August 2, 2010.

Rossi, Rosalind. "The Woman behind Obama." *Chicago Sun-Times*, January 20, 2007.

Ruane, Michael. "D.C.'s Inauguration Head Count: 1.2 Million." *The Washington Post*, January 20, 2009.

Scharnberg, Kirsten, and Kim Barker. "The Not-So-Simple Story of Barack Obama's Youth." *Chicago Tribune*, March 25, 2007.

Schear, Michael D. "Obama Gets to Test His Game Against Hoops Greats." *The Washington Post*, August 9, 2010.

Shear, Michael. "Health Law Delivers on Promises, With Notable Failings, in First Year." *The New York Times*, October 27, 2014.

———. "For Obama, more audacity and fulfillment of languishing promises." *The New York Times*, December 18, 2014.

Scott, Janny. "A Free-Spirited Wanderer Who Set Obama's Path." *The New York Times*, March 14, 2008.

———. "The Story of Obama, Written by Obama." *The New York Times*, May 18, 2008.

SOURCES

Slevin, Peter. "Obama Says He Regrets Land Deal With Fundraiser." *The Washington Post*, December 17, 2006.

Spillius, Alex. "Barack Obama Health Care Speech: Republican Calls President a Liar." *The Telegraph*, September 10, 2009.

Sullivan, Amy. "The Obamas Find a Church Home—Away from Home." *Time*, June 29, 2009.

Superville, Darlene. "Malia Obama Looks Forward to Decorating WH Room." *The Associated Press*, July 7, 2008.

Swarns, Rachel L. "And the Winner Is . . . Sidwell Friends." *The New York Times*, November 21, 2008.

Sweet, Lynne. "Obama July 22, 2009, Press Conference." *The Chicago Sun-Times*, July 22, 2009.

Toobin, Jeffrey. "The Obama Brief," *The New Yorker*, October 27, 2014, pp. 24–32.

Travis, Shannon. "Quarter Doubt Obama Was Born in U.S." CNN Poll, August 4, 2010.

USA Today. "Obama, in Gulf, Pledges to Push on Stopping Leak." May 28, 2010.

Vinik, Danny. "Obama's first counterattack: Executive action on immigration." *The New Republic*, November 6, 2014.

Viser, Matt. "Activity links commanders in chief." *The Boston Globe*, August 8, 2014, p. D11.

Walsh, Declan; Adams, Richard; and McAskill, Ewan. "Osama bin Laden Is Dead, Obama Announces." *The Guardian*, May 1, 2011.

Wickham, DeWayne. "The reason Obama backers should 'stop crying'? His judiciary appointments." *USA Today*, September 27, 2011, p. 9A.

SOURCES

VIDEOS

"Barack Obama." A&E Biography, 2005.

"Maya Soetoro-Ng, Barack's Sister." YouTube interview. Uploaded February 13, 2008. http://www.youtube.com/watch?v=7m4didWsPKE

Senator Obama Goes to Africa. Directed by Bob Hercules, 2007.

INTERNET

Official Barack Obama website. www.barackobama.com

Abdullah, Halimah. "Not in my backyard: Communities protest surge of immigrant kids." http://edition.cnn.com/2014/07/15/politics /immigration-not-in-my-backyard/index.html?iid=article_sidebar

Baker, Peter, and Davis, Julie Hirschfield. "Obama, down but not out, presses ahead." http://www.nytimes.com/2014/11/14/us/politics/down -but-not-out-obama-presses-ahead.html

Bartash, Jeffrey. "US adds 214,000 jobs in October to take jobless rate to 6-year low." http://www.marketwatch.com/story/us-gains-214000 -jobs-in-october-unemployment-drops-to-58-2014-11-07

Bolton, Alexander. "Centrist Republicans cool to minimum wage hike compromise." http://thehill.com/homenews/senate/202641-centrist -republicans-cool-to-wage-compromise

Centers for Disease Control and Prevention. "Progress on Childhood Obesity." August 2013. http://www.cdc.gov/vitalsigns/childhoodobesity/

Clawson, Laura. "Fast food workers strike in 60 cities." http://www.dailykos .com/story/2013/08/29/1234750/-Fast-food-workers-strike-in-60-cities#

Daly, Corbett. "Obama Backs Same-Sex Marriage." May 2012. http:// www.cbsnews.com/news/obama-backs-same-sex-marriage/

The Economist. "Out of the shadows: a first step to make young immigrants welcome." August 25, 2012. http://www.economist.com/node /21560900

Epstein, Jennifer. "Chicago tops list of Obama library finalists." http://www.politico.com/story/2014/09/barack-obama-presidential-library-chicago-110970.html

Gabriel, Trip, and Fernandez, Manny. "Voter ID laws scrutinized for impact on midterms." http://www.nytimes.com/2014/11/19/us/voter-id-laws-midterm-elections.html?_r=0

Gallup polls. "Barack Obama presidential job approval." http://www.gallup.com/poll/116479/barack-obama-presidential-job-approval.aspx

Gambino, Lauren. "Immigration crisis forces Obama to 'act alone' with executive orders." http://www.theguardian.com/world/2014/aug/04/us-immigration-obama-executive-order-options-deportation

Goldberg, Jeffrey. "Obama: 'Israel doesn't know what its best interests are.'" http://archive.peacenow.org/entries/jeffrey_goldberg-_obama_israel_doesnt_know_what_its_best_interests_are

Horsley, Scott, NPR. "Enrollment jumps at Healthcare.gov, though totals still lag." http://www.npr.org/blogs/health/2013/12/11/250023704/enrollment-jumps-at-healthcare-gov-though-totals-still-lag

Jackson, David. "Obama: 1B program for early childhood education." http://www.usatoday.com/story/theoval/2014/12/10/obama-early-childhood-education-summit-1-billion/20201721/

———. "Obama, Christie laud 'working relationship' on storm." http://www.usatoday.com/story/news/politics/2012/10/31/christie-obama-hurricane-sandy-new-jersey/1671787/

———. "Obama: Income inequality threatens American dream." http://www.usatoday.com/story/news/politics/2013/12/04/obama-income-inequality-speech-center-for-american-progress/3867747/

Kaplan, Rebecca. "Obama on Ferguson follow-up: 'This time will be different.'" http://www.cbsnews.com/news/obama-on-ferguson-follow-up-this-time-will-be-different/

Neuhauser, Alan. "Obama Charges Ahead on Climate Change Policy." http://www.usnews.com/news/articles/2014/08/27/obama-charges-ahead-on-climate-change-policy

SOURCES

Nichols, John. "Obama's 3 Million Vote, Electoral College Landslide, Majority of States Mandate." http://www.thenation.com/blog/171178/obama-has-great-big-mandate-and-he-must-use-it#

Obama, Barack. Remarks at press conference, November 5, 2014. https://www.whitehouse.gov/the-press-office/2014/11/05/remarks-president-press-conference

———. State of the Union speech, February 12, 2013. https://www.whitehouse.gov/state-of-the-union-2013

———. State of the Union speech 2013. http://www.whitehouse.gov/photos-and-video/video/2013/02/14/president-obama-early-childhood-education

Pengelly, Martin. "Arab nations join Syria strikes as Nusra front threatens retaliation." http://www.theguardian.com/world/2014/sep/27/obama-us-isis-syria-iraq-coalition-kurds-jets-strike

Pew Research Center. "New Poll: Public Wants EPA to Do More to Reduce Air Pollution." http://www.lung.org/about-us/our-impact/top-stories/new-poll-epa-air-pollution.html?referrer=https://www.google.com/

Preston, Mark. "Poll: Americans back airstrikes, but oppose use of US troops in Iraq, Syria." http://www.cnn.com/2014/09/29/politics/poll-americans-back-airstrikes/

Reiff, Laura Foote. "US Senate passes landmark comprehensive immigration reform legislation." http://www.natlawreview.com/article/us-senate-passes-landmark-comprehensive-immigration-reform-legislation

Reeves, Richard V. "2014 Midterms: Inequality Lurks Beneath the Surface." http://tinyurl.com/ptoonwy

Saad, Lydia. "One in Six Say Immigration Most Important U.S. Problem." http://www.gallup.com/poll/173306/one-six-say-immigration-important-problem.aspx

Saez, Emmanuel. "Striking It Richer: The Evolution of Top Incomes in the United States." http://eml.berkeley.edu/~saez/saez-UStopincomes-2012.pdf

SOURCES

Sapiro, Miriam. "Obama heads to Asia for APEC, ASEAN, EAS and the G-20." http://www.brookings.edu/blogs/up-front/posts/2014/11/07-strengthen -global-trade-g20-summit-sapiro?utm_campaign=Brookings+Brief&utm _source=hs_email&utm_medium=email&utm_co

Scherer, Michael. "2012 Person of the Year: Barack Obama, the President." http://poy.time.com/2012/12/19/person-of-the-year-barack-obama/

Shen, Aviva. "Michelle Obama Derided for Being a Feminist Nightmare." http://thinkprogress.org/health/2013/11/22/2983381/michelle-obama -feminism-womens-work/

Smith, Matt, and Tom Cohen, CNN. "No 'sugar-coating' problems with health web site." http://edition.cnn.com/2013/10/21/politics/obamacare -problems/

Tapper, Jake. "Obama announces 34,000 troops to come home." http:// www.cnn.com/2011/POLITICS/06/22/afghanistan.troops.drawdown/

Traynor, Ian, and Lewis, Paul. "Merkel compared NSA to Stasi in heated encounter with Obama. http://www.theguardian.com/world/2013 /dec/17/merkel-compares-nsa-stasi-obama

Tritch, Teresa. "F.D.R. Makes the Case for the Minimum Wage." http:// takingnote.blogs.nytimes.com/2014/03/07/f-d-r-makes-the-case-for -the-minimum-wage/?_php=true&_type=blogs&_r=0

United States Department of Labor, Bureau of Labor Statistics, September 2014. http://data.bls.gov/timeseries/LNS14000000

US casualties in Afghanistan War touch 2000. http://www.rediff.com /news/report/us-casualties-in-afghanistan-war-touch-2000/20121001 .htm

The Week staff. "Abu Bakr al-Baghdadi: The man who would be caliph." http://theweek.com/article/index/267920/abu-bakr-al-baghdadi-the -man-who-would-be-caliph

SOURCES

SPEECHES

Obama, Barack. "Keynote Address at the 2004 Democratic National Convention." Boston, MA, July 27, 2004. http://www.pbs.org/newshour /vote2004/demconvention/speeches/obama.html

—————. "A More Perfect Union." Speech on race in America at the National Constitution Center, Philadelphia, PA, March 18, 2008. http:// my.barackobama.com/page/content/hisownwords

—————. President Barack Obama's Inaugural Address. Washington, D.C., January 21, 2009. http://www.whitehouse.gov/blog/inaugural-address/

—————. "Remarks by the President at the Acceptance of the Nobel Peace Prize," December 10, 2009. http://www.whitehouse.gov/the -press-office/remarks-president-acceptance-nobel-peace-prize

—————. "Remarks of State Senator Barack Obama against Going to War with Iraq." Speech for an antiwar rally, Chicago, IL, October 2, 2002. http://www.npr.org/templates/story/story.php?storyId=99591469

—————. "Remarks on His Birth Certificate." April 21, 2011. http:// www.whitehouse.gov/the-press-office/2011/04/27/remarks-president

—————. "Senator Barack Obama's Announcement for President." Spring- field, IL, February 10, 2007. http://www.nytimes.com/2007/02/10/us /politics/11obama-text.html?pagewanted=all

—————. Speech on December 6, 2011, in Osawatomie, Kansas.

"American Recovery and Reinvestment Act of 2009," DonsList.net, February 19, 2009. http://news.bbc.co.uk/2/hi/business/7889897.stm

"Barack Obama Pictures: The Early Years," ChicagoTribune.com. http://www.chicagotribune.com/news/politics/070323obama-early -photogallery,0,5458360.photogallery

"BP Oil Still Ashore One Year After End of Gulf Spill," by Jim Polson. Bloomberg.com, July 15, 2011. http://www.bloomberg.com/news/2011 -07-15/bp-oil-still-washing-ashore-one-year-after-end-of-gulf-spill.html

SOURCES

"Chances of Closing Guantanamo Jail Very Low: Gates," Reuters.com, February 17, 2011. http://www.reuters.com/article/2011/02/17/us-usa-guantanamo-idUSTRE71G4NG20110217

"Final Vote Results for Roll Call 70: Making Supplemental Appropriations for Fiscal Year Ending 2009," Office of the Clerk, U.S. House of Representatives. February 13, 2009. http://clerk.house.gov/evs/2009/roll070.xml

"Final Vote Results for Roll Call 165: Patient Protection and Affordable Care Act. Office of the Clerk, U.S. House of Representatives. March 21, 2010. http://clerk.house.gov/evs/2010/roll165.xml

"GOP Quick to Release 'Repeal' Bills," TheHill.com, March 22, 2010. http://thehill.com/blogs/blog-briefing-room/news/88323-house-and-senate-republicans-quick-to-release-repeal-bills

"In U.S., Significantly Fewer 18- to 25-Year-Olds Uninsured," by Elizabeth Mendes.Gallup.com, September 21, 2011. http://www.gallup.com/poll/149558/significantly-fewer-year-olds-uninsured.aspx

"Income, Poverty, and Health Insurance Coverage in the United States: 2009, Issued September 2010." http://www.census.gov/prod/2010pubs/p60-238.pdf

"Key Powers Reach Compromise at Climate Summit," BBC.com, December 19, 2009. http://news.bbc.co.uk/2/hi/europe/8421935.stm

"Morning Fix: Six Senators To Watch On Health Care," by Chris Cillizza. WashingtonPost.com, June 16, 2009. http://voices.washingtonpost.com/thefix/morning-fix/061609-morning-fix.html

"NATO to Police Libya No-Fly Zone," Aljazeera.com, March 25, 2011. http://english.aljazeera.net/news/africa/2011/03/2011324221036894697.html

"Obama Decision on Afghanistan Troop Withdrawal to Come Soon," by Kristen Welker. First Read on MSNBC.com, June 6, 2011. http://firstread.msnbc.msn.com/_news/2011/06/06/6798666-obama-decision-on-afghanistan-troop-withdrawal-to-come-soon

SOURCES

"Obama Details Afghan War Plan, Troop Increases," by The Associated Press.

MSNBC.com, December 1, 2009. http://www.msnbc.msn.com/id /34218604/ns/politics-white_house

"Obama in Egypt Reaches Out to Muslim World," CNN.com, June 4, 2009, http://articles.cnn.com/2009-06-04/politics/egypt.obama.speech_1 _muslim-israeli-settlements-palestinians?_s=PM:POLITICS

"Obama: No Offshore Drilling in East Coast Waters," by The Associated Press. MSNBC.com, December 1, 2010. http://www.msnbc.msn.com /id/40455797/ns/us _news-environment/t/obama-no-offshore-drilling -east-coast-waters/#.TsF8DFa25Og

"Obama, Russian President Sign Arms Treaty," by the CNN Wire staff. CNN.com, April 8, 2010. http://articles.cnn.com/2010-04-08/politics /obama.russia.treaty_1_nuclear-weapons-nuclear-non-proliferation -treaty-nuclear-arms?_s=PM:POLITICS

"Obama Signs Defense Authorization Bill," by Jared Serbu. 1500 AM FederalNewsRadio.com, January 7, 2011. http://www.federalnewsradio .com/?nid=741&sid=2226350

"Obama Views Children's Health Bill as Step One," by The Associated Press. MSNBC.com, February 5, 2009. http://www.msnbc.msn.com /id/29011620/

"Senate Votes to Block Funds for Guantanamo Closure," by Andrew Taylor. The Associated Press, May 20, 2009. http://www.guardian.co.uk- /world/feedarticle/8517686

"Statement by Dr. Chiyome Fukino," Department of Health News Release, October 31, 2008. http://hawaii.gov/health/about/pr/2008/08-93.pdf

"US Congress Passes Stimulus Plan," BBC.com, February 14, 2009. http://news.bbc.co.uk/2/hi/business/7889897.stm

"World Health Statistics 2009," © World Health Organization 2009. http://www.who.int/whosis/whostat/2009/en/index.html

INDEX

INDEX